Immortality for Entrepreneurs

Immortality for Entrepreneurs

Dr. John H. Roller

Immortality for Entrepreneurs
Copyright © 2015 by Dr. John H. Roller

ISBN 978-1-943767-01-4
ISBN 978-1-943767-02-1
ISBN 978-1-943767-03-8

Inquiries regarding permission for use of material contained in this book should be addressed to the publisher:

The Ethics Institute
11027-105 Guildwood Parkway
Scarborough, Ontario M1E 1P1
Canada

www.ethicsinstitute.ca

Contents

Foreword

I highly recommend this book to all Certified General Ethicists (CGEs), and every entrepreneur.

There is currently a trend that implies everyone will succeed just by willing something to happen. In Canada there is a television advertisement that goes something like this:

"I will discover a cure for cancer by 2025," says an eager-looking student who is considering going to a tertiary level institution. Simply getting the right education does not mean that this person **will** discover a cure for cancer by 2025.

Entrepreneurs are not immune to this kind of thinking. If any of you have seen either *Shark Tank* or *Dragons' Den*, you have seen many entrepreneurs (who are sometimes referred to as "wantrepreneurs") who have no sales but want venture capitalists to invest thousands of dollars in their dream.

Dr. John H. Roller is a friend (for decades) and colleague in the Association of Certified General Ethicists, where he serves as Vice-President.

This is an exceptional case study of a Christian denomination that strived to catch the wave of church planting. Many megachurches were founded, and some died, as a result of the church planting movement.

This book is a combination of two works by Dr. John H. Roller.

Part I Data consists of Dr. Roller's doctoral thesis, *Immortality in the Early Church*.

Part II Application consists of Dr. Roller's paper, *Advent Christian Church Efforts 1950-1980.*

Part III Consequences evaluates what every entrepreneur and professional can learn from these experiences as documented by Dr. Roller. Theanthropic Ethics© offers to reinvigorate any business, enterprise (including a Christian denomination), or profession.

This is particularly of interest to any CGE or any other professional who is committed to Reinvigorating any enterprise or business through the Truth.

Dr. Brian Keen, CGE
President and CEO of The Ethics Institute

Note to the Reader

This book is a work in progress. It began as my PhD thesis when I was a student at Bethany Theological Seminary in Dothan, Alabama. Later, it was revised and expanded while I was working as Resource Center Coordinator for the Advent Christian General Conference in Charlotte, North Carolina. In 2005, it became the textbook for an intensive course that I taught at Atlanta Bible College in Morrow, Georgia. Some of the students who took that course wrote papers that were so good that I asked them for permission to include their work in future editions. Two of those were Becky Onyango, whose paper on Justin of Samaria included references to books that I hadn't yet read by then, and Dustin Smith, whose paper on Justin of Samaria steered me to several references in Justin's writings that I hadn't previously noticed. Anne Mbeke's paper on Clement of Alexandria was so good that I helped her publish it and made several references to it in the later editions of my chapter on that author. Brian Wright wrote a paper on the "Odes of Solomon" that became an entire chapter (see below).

The present edition was updated in 2015.

If you have any comments on this material or suggestions for improvement, please contact me. I will gladly consider your comments or suggestions for possible inclusion in future editions. Should any of your ideas be implemented, I will gladly exchange this copy for a copy of the new version, at no additional cost to you. You can reach me through the publisher.

It is my prayer that reading this book will stimulate you to further and more extensive study on this interesting and important topic.

Part I
Data

Introduction

Most modern evangelical Christians believe that every human being has within him (or her) a naturally immortal soul which, being separated from the body at the moment of physical death, continues to exist forever, either in the enjoyment of God's presence or in the everlasting torment of hellfire—in the latter case, in particular, consciously experiencing the pain of burning, but never actually being burnt up.

This position is well stated by the popular evangelist, Dr. Billy Graham, in his book, *Peace with God,* chapter 6, paragraph 25, where he says, "The Bible teaches that you are an immortal soul. Your soul is eternal and will live forever. In other words, the real you—the part of you that thinks, feels, dreams, aspires; the ego, the personality—will never die. The Bible teaches that your soul will live forever in one of two places—heaven or hell."

In the same chapter, in paragraph 28, he adds, "The Bible teaches that whether we are saved or lost, there is conscious and everlasting existence of the soul and personality."

This belief is actually written into the Statements of Faith of many Protestant denominations—for example, the Southern Baptist Convention, the Assemblies of God, the General Association of Regular Baptist Churches, the American Baptist Association, the International Church of the Foursquare Gospel, and the Evangelical Free Church of America (to name just a few). Thus it is held to be both Biblically supportable and doctrinally essential by those churches that so include it.

On the other hand, a small but vocal minority, who refer to themselves as "Conditionalists," believe that the soul (by which term they mean, the "whole personality") is naturally mortal, not immortal, and consequently cannot, and will not, live forever (in any condition) unless immortality is granted to the individual by God—and that God only grants immortality to those who trust in Jesus Christ as their personal Savior and follow Him as their Lord.

This position is well stated by Dr. David A. Dean, of Berkshire Christian College, in his book, *Resurrection Hope*, on page 83, where he says, "Nothing in the Bible teaches that the wicked are immortal. Such expressions as 'to live forever,' 'to exist forever,' 'never to die,' 'to be immortal,' nor any equivalent expressions, are ever applied to the nature of the soul, or the destiny of the lost. They are only applied to the destiny of the righteous. Death is the inevitable wages for sin. Eternal life is God's gift to only those who believe in Jesus Christ."

In the same book, on page 84, he adds, "The second death destroys the whole person completely and irreversibly. Jesus said, 'Do not be afraid of those who kill the body but cannot kill the soul. Rather, be afraid of the One who can destroy both soul and body in hell' (Matt. 10:28). In the second death there is a complete and never-ending destruction of the total personality (or personhood) of the sinner. One's life is taken away and eternal life is withheld."

This doctrine is called, by those who hold it, "Conditional Immortality," and those who believe it have often been driven to form churches and denominations of their own—for example, the Seventh-Day Adventist Church, the Advent Christian General Conference of America, the Christadelphian Church, the Church of God of the Abrahamic Faith (and others)—because they feel unable honestly to sign the Statements of Faith of other churches, such as those previously mentioned.

In my opinion, however, the beliefs of present-day churches are no valid standard by which to judge the truth or falsehood of any doctrine. We are now almost as far removed in the stream of time from Christ and the Apostles as Abraham was before God spoke to him in Mesopotamia—and God has not spoken to anyone, by way of inspired revelation, in over nineteen centuries! On the question of human immortality, as on every other subject of spiritual interest, we should not ask, "What do modern churches teach?" but rather, "What does the Bible say?" and "How did the early Christians interpret its statements?"

With this principle in mind, then, the topic for this book is defined as follows: what can we learn from the writings of the early Church Fathers as to the position(s) held in their times on the subject of human immortality? Specifically, we will want to see whether the Apostolic, Subapostolic, and Ante-Nicene Fathers of the first, second, and third centuries held a view similar to the popular modern view, or one more similar to the Conditionalist view.

Chapter 1
Natural Immortality

Proponents of the view I am referring to as the doctrine of "Natural Immortality," or "Naturalism," usually hold either a dichotomist or trichotomist view of the nature of man.[1] Let me define these two terms.

Dichotomism is the view that a human being consists of two separable parts, the "material" and the "immaterial." In this view, the "material part" consists of everything that can be observed and analyzed chemically: in other words, the "body." The "immaterial part" consists of everything that cannot be so observed and analyzed: the "mind," the "emotions," the "personality," and the "soul," or "spirit" (most dichotomists use the latter two terms almost interchangeably).

Trichotomism, on the other hand, is the view that a human being consists of three separable parts, the "body," the "soul," and the "spirit." In this view, the "body" consists of everything that can be observed and analyzed chemically, and the "soul" and the "spirit" are distinguished, not only from the "body," but also from each other. The "soul" is usually viewed as that "part" of man which is immaterial, but is also possessed by animals (the "mind," the "emotions," etc.), while the "spirit" is that "part" of man which is both immaterial and uniquely human (the "will," the "personality," the ability to make moral choices, the ability to have a relationship with God, etc.).

Both dichotomists and trichotomists believe that at death, the "parts" are separated and experience different destinies. Dichotomists and trichotomists agree that the "material part," or "body," disintegrates unless chemically or miraculously preserved; dichotomists believe that the "immaterial part" survives, remains

---

[1] See, for example, the discussion of "The Nature of Man" in Charles Ryrie, *A Survey of Bible Doctrine*, Chicago: Moody Press, 1972, 104–107.

conscious, and goes directly to its eternal destiny, while trichotomists believe that the "soul" and the "spirit" are separated, not only from the "body," but also from each other, and may experience separate, and different, destinies.

For the purposes of this book, I will not attempt to distinguish between dichotomists and trichotomists, but will lump into one group all those who believe that a human being consists of separable parts, if they hold in common the idea that some "part" of man survives the death of the "body" and is destined before Creation to continue to exist forever. These people I will conveniently designate as "Naturalists," meaning that they hold to the view I am referring to as the doctrine of "Natural Immortality," or "Naturalism." (The terms "Naturalist" and "Naturalism," as used in this context, should not be confused with the terms "Naturalist" and "Naturalism" as used in the context of people enjoying outdoor activities, organically grown foods, nudity, and so on.)

Chapter 2
Conditional Immortality

Proponents of the view I am referring to as the doctrine of "Conditional Immortality," or "Conditionalism," usually hold a monistic, or "unitary," view of the nature of man.[2] Here is another term to define.

In this view, the "body," "soul," "spirit," and so on, are not separable "parts," but merely different ways of describing the same individual person. The "body" is the person viewed from a physical standpoint; the "mind" is the person viewed from an intellectual standpoint; the "will" is the person viewed in his or her capacity to make moral choices; and so on.

Adherents to this doctrine see the term "soul" as equivalent to the "total personality," pointing to the many references in Scripture where the expression "my soul" is used to mean "I," "his soul," "he," etc. And, for many who hold this view, the "spirit" is not seen as an aspect of the human being at all, but as the "living force" which "energizes" the person and makes him (or her) "alive" (as opposed to "dead").

It should seem logical to you, as it does to me, that anyone holding such a view of the nature of man will not view death as any kind of "separation" of the human being into "parts" with differing destinies. This definition of man's nature requires that every aspect of his total personality experience the same fate. Since the fate of at least one aspect—the "body"—is well known to be disintegration (and eventual nonexistence), it should be obvious that the fate of all the other aspects would be the same, and that there would be no hope for a person's

---

[2] See, for example, Basil Atkinson's discussion of "The Nature of Man" in his book, *Life and Immortality*, Taunton: Phoenix Press, undated, 1–29. Note also the opening paragraph of his Introduction on iii.

continued existence, in any form, after his (or her) death, unless God were to intervene with a miracle.

That is, indeed, what most Conditionalists believe, based on their understanding of the nature of human beings. The idea of "**Conditional** Immortality" is then introduced as the solution to the problem thus created. According to this view, God will raise whole persons from a state of death to a state of immortality, providing that, in this life, the "**condition**" (faith in Christ as Lord and Savior) has been met. Those who have not believed in Christ will be punished with the "second," or final, death: complete destruction of the entire person, or "soul," with no hope of another opportunity for repentance and salvation. Though many Conditionalists dislike the word "annihilation," it accurately describes what they believe will be the ultimate fate of those who do not repent of their sins—in this life—and receive God's forgiveness.

In this book, I will conveniently designate as "Conditionalists" those writers who hold to the view I am referring to as the doctrine of "Conditional Immortality," or "Conditionalism."

Chapter 3

The Ancient Sources

As mentioned in the Introduction (see above), our primary source of data on the understanding of human immortality that prevailed in the Early Church will be the writings of the Apostolic, Subapostolic, and Ante-Nicene Fathers of the first, second, and third centuries (AD). These are defined as follows:

1) The Apostolic Fathers are those writers whose lifetimes overlapped with those of the Apostles, and who may therefore be supposed to have had personal knowledge of the Apostles' teachings.

2) The Subapostolic Fathers are those writers whose lifetimes overlapped with those of the Apostolic Fathers, and who may therefore be supposed to have had personal knowledge of the Apostolic Fathers' understanding of the Apostles' teachings.

3) The Ante-Nicene Fathers are all other Christian writers whose work was completed before the Council of Nicaea, which took place AD 325.

Since Apostle John died AD 102, I will classify as Apostolic Fathers only those writers born before that date. Of this group, those who wrote on the subject of immortality were:

Clement of Rome (AD 30–97)
The writer(s) of the *Odes of Solomon* (approximately AD 100)
Ignatius of Antioch (AD 35–107)
Polycarp of Smyrna (AD 69–155)
Papias of Hierapolis (AD 70–163)
The writer(s) of the *Didache* (approximately AD 120)
Quadratus of Athens (approximately AD 126)

"Mathetes" (approximately AD 130)
Clement of Corinth (approximately AD 130)
Barnabas of Alexandria (approximately AD 135)
Aristides of Athens (approximately AD 140)
Hermas of Rome (AD 100–?)

Based on these dates, I will use AD 142 (a generation after the death of Apostle John) as a convenient cutoff date to distinguish between the Subapostolic Fathers and the Ante-Nicene Fathers; that is, writers born after AD 102 but before AD 142 will be classified as Subapostolic. The Subapostolic Fathers, then, who wrote on the subject of immortality, were:

Justin of Samaria (AD 106–165)
Tatian of Assyria (AD 110–180)
Theophilus of Antioch (AD 115–181)
Melito of Sardis (AD ?–190)
Athenagoras of Athens (AD 127–190)
Polycrates of Ephesus (AD 125–196)
Irenaeus of Lyons (AD 130–202)

And, by these definitions, the Ante-Nicene Fathers who wrote on the subject of immortality before the end of the third century AD were:

Clement of Alexandria (AD 153–213?)
Tertullian of Carthage (AD 145–220)
Hippolytus of Portus Romanus (AD 170–236)
The writer(s) of the *Pseudo–Clementines* (approximately AD 220)
Minucius Felix of Africa (AD 185–250)
Origen of Alexandria (AD 185–254)
Commodianus of Africa (AD 200–275)
Cyprian of Carthage (AD 200–258)
Novatian of Rome (AD 210–280)
Gregory Thaumaturgus of Neocaesarea (AD 213–270)
Arnobius of Sicca (AD 250–327)

This is not, of course, a complete list of all the Christian writers of the first three centuries (AD); however, it is a complete list of all those writers of that period in whose works I was able to find any reference to the subject of human immortality. In any case, no major Christian writers of the first three centuries have been intentionally omitted from consideration in the compiling of this list. It cannot be said that I have begged the question to be discussed in this book by prejudiced selection of source materials.

Chapter 4
The Ancient Sources Consulted

The Biblical texts relating to the question of human immortality are far too numerous to list and evaluate in a book of this length; nor is it the purpose of this book to "prove" the correctness or incorrectness of the doctrines of Naturalism and Conditionalism by the traditional method of Scriptural proof-texting. It is, rather, the stated purpose of this book to determine which of the two positions was more prominent in the Christian Church during its first three centuries of existence. For this reason I will purposely avoid any attempts to analyze the writings of the Apostles themselves, or any other Scriptures, and restrict our attention to an examination of the teachings of the Apostolic, Subapostolic, and Ante-Nicene Fathers. My procedure will be as follows:

In approximately chronological order, I will describe each writer in a brief biography; list his major works, together with their dates of publication, if known; then analyze some quotations from his writings, using **bold face** type to emphasize key words, with a view to determining if he should be classified as a Naturalist or a Conditionalist. Since only a few pages will be given to each Father, it should be obvious that this will not be a verse-by-verse study of all of the Patristic writings! But it will represent the conclusions drawn from careful, in-depth study of each Father and his works, and I will try my best to be unbiased in my attempts at classification. It is my belief that the point to be made in the conclusion can best be established by this method.

The Apostolic Fathers

As mentioned above, the Apostolic Fathers who wrote on the subject of human immortality are:

Clement of Rome (AD 30–97)
The writer(s) of the *Odes of Solomon* (approximately AD 100)
Ignatius of Antioch (AD 35–107)
Polycarp of Smyrna (AD 69–155)
Papias of Hierapolis (AD 70–163)
The writer(s) of the *Didache* (approximately AD 120)
Quadratus of Athens (approximately AD 126)
"Mathetes" (approximately AD 130)
Clement of Corinth (approximately AD 130)
Barnabas of Alexandria (approximately AD 135)
Aristides of Athens (approximately AD 140)
Hermas of Rome (AD 100–?)

Their writings cover approximately the first half of the second century.

Clement of Rome

Clement was born approximately AD 30; we do not know where. Origen of Alexandria (AD 185–254) says that he was the Clement mentioned by Apostle Paul when he wrote, "And I intreat thee also, true yokefellow, help those women which labored with me in the gospel, with Clement also, and with other my fellowlaborers, whose names are in the book of life," (Philippians 4:3). He was ordained to the ministry by Apostle Peter. According to Eusebius of Caesarea (AD 263–339), who is known as the "Father of Church History," he served as the fourth Bishop of Rome from AD 88–97.[3] He was exiled to Crimea during the persecution instigated by the famous Roman Emperor Trajan, and was martyred there, by drowning.

Clement's *Epistle to the Corinthians*, commonly known as *1 Clement*, is the oldest specimen of post-Apostolic literature we now

---

[3] Mark Hoffman, *1989 World Almanac*, New York: Pharos Books, 1988, 509.

possess. It was written about AD 95[4] and was "read in numerous churches (in Eusebius' time), as being almost on a level with the canonical writings."

1 Clement contains several references to immortality and the final destiny of the wicked. For example:

1 Clement 26:1 asks, "Do we then deem it any great and wonderful thing for the Maker of all things to **raise up again those that have piously served Him** in the assurance of a good faith...?" (implying that God will **not** "raise up again" those who have not so served Him).

1 Clement 30:7 quotes *Job* 14:1 as saying, "He that is born of woman ... **lives** but a **short** time" (as opposed to living forever) (a rather free, but essentially accurate, quotation). The rest of the chapter is a favorite text of many modern Conditionalists, including such statements as, "Man lieth down, and riseth not: till the heavens be no more, they shall not awake, nor be raised out of their sleep" (Job 14:12); "If a man die, shall he live again? all the days of my appointed time will I wait, till my change come" (Job 14:14); and "the mountain falling cometh to nought, and the rock is removed out of his place. The waters wear the stones: thou washest away the things which grow out of the dust of the earth; and thou destroyest the hope of man." (Job 14:18–19).

1 Clement 35:1–2 presents "Life in immortality" as one of "the **gifts** of God" (not as a natural possession of human beings). The full text reads, "How blessed and wonderful, beloved, are the gifts of God! Life in immortality, splendor in righteousness, truth in boldness, faith in confidence, continence in holiness: and all these things are submitted to our understanding."[5]

---

[4]   LeRoy Froom, *The Conditionalist Faith of Our Fathers*, Washington: Review and Herald Publishing, 1966, 762.

[5]   Kirsopp Lake, *The Apostolic Fathers*, Cambridge: Harvard University Press, 1965, 67.

1 Clement 36:2 says, "By Him (Jesus) the Lord has willed that **we** should taste of [the knowledge of immortality]." The context makes it clear that the word "we" refers only to the saved, not to the unsaved—implying that the latter will **not** "taste of [the knowledge of immortality]."

1 Clement 39:2 asks, "For what can a **mortal** man do, or what strength is there in one made out of the dust?" Here Clement refers to man as "**mortal**" (not "immortal") and describes him as "one made out of the dust," which may indicate that Clement held the "materialist" form of the monistic or "unitary" view of the nature of man.[6]

1 Clement 41:3 says, "Those, therefore, who do anything beyond that which is agreeable to His (i.e., God's) will, are punished with **death** (not 'torment')."[7]

1 Clement 44:2 refers to the apostles as having appointed ministers and having given "instructions, that when these should **fall asleep** (the favorite Conditionalist phrase to describe death), other approved men should succeed them in their ministry."

1 Clement 48:1–2 refers to "brotherly love" as "the gate of righteousness … for the attainment of **life**" (implying that those who do not have this love have not walked through this "gate" and thus do not have everlasting "life").

1 Clement 50:3 says that, "All the generations from Adam even unto this day have passed away; but **those who**, through the grace of God, have been made perfect in love, **now possess a place among the godly**, and **shall be made manifest at the revelation of the kingdom** of Christ." The next verse, in an attempt to back up this statement, quotes *Isaiah* 26:20 as saying, "Enter into thy secret chambers for a little time, until my wrath and fury pass away; and I will remember a

---

6   Lake, *op. cit.*
7   *Ibid.*, 79.

propitious day, and will **raise you up out of your graves**." This first half of this quotation is a substantially accurate summary of *Isaiah* 26:20, but the second half is not found in our present text of that verse, and should therefore be understood as Clement's own "interpretation" of what *Isaiah* was saying. In the process of giving that interpretation, Clement has shown us he believes the "place" of the departed "godly" to be their "graves" (until "the revelation of the kingdom" occurs). Thus it is clear he did **not** believe the righteous "go to Heaven" when they die!

1 Clement 51:5 says that "Pharaoh and his army and all the rulers of Egypt, 'the chariots and their riders,' were sunk in the Red Sea, and **perished** for no other cause than that their foolish hearts were hardened, after signs and wonders had been wrought in the land of Egypt by God's servant Moses."[8] The Greek word here translated "perished" is *apolonto,* which literally means "**destroyed**"—not "tormented."

1 Clement 53:4 quotes the Lord (in Exodus 32:10) as saying, "Let me **destroy** (not "torment") them, and **blot out their name from under heaven**" (a nicely "pictorial" way of saying "make them completely nonexistent"). But, again, these words are not found in our present text of Exodus, and must be understood as Clement's own interpretation of the word translated "consume" in Exodus 32:10. Similarly, the next verse (*1 Clement* 53:5) quotes Moses (in *Exodus* 32:32) as saying, "**Blot** me also **out of the book of the living**." But our present text of *Exodus* 32:32 reads, "Blot me, I pray thee, out of **thy book which thou hast written**." Notice how Clement interprets God's "book!" The passage concludes (in *1 Clement* 53:6) with the statement that, "The servant (i.e., Moses) speaks freely to his Lord, and asks forgiveness for the people, or begs that he himself might **perish** (see comment on *1 Clement* 51:5) along with them."

---

8   *Ibid.*, 97.

1 Clement 56:16 predicts the reader's death by saying, "Thou shalt **come to the grave**" (not "go to Heaven").

1 Clement 57:4–10 quotes "Wisdom" (*Proverbs* 1:20) as saying, in *Proverbs* 1:26, "I too will laugh at your **destruction**" (*The Holy Bible* Authorized Version (AV), commonly referred to as the King James Version (KJV), translates this word in this context, as "calamity"), and, in *Proverbs* 1:32–33, "For, in punishment for the wrongs which they practiced upon babes, shall they be **slain** (not "tormented"), and inquiry will be **death** (in this case, *The Holy Bible* (AV—KJV) uses the word "destroy" at this point) to the ungodly; but he that heareth me shall rest in hope and be undisturbed by the fear of any evil."

Again, *1 Clement* 59:1 describes God as the one "who (among other things) '**destroyest**' the calculations of the heathen"—quoting Psalm 33:10, which reads, "The LORD bringeth the counsel of the heathen to nought: he maketh the devices of the people of none effect." Evidently Clement believed that to "destroy" something was the same as "bringing" it to "nought," or reducing it to nonexistence.

Clement **never** uses the terms "immortal soul" or "immortality of the soul"[9] and never speaks of a process of punishment that goes on and on throughout eternity. "Clement clearly believed that immortality was conditional—to be bestowed on the righteous only."[10]

The Writer(s) of the *Odes of Solomon*

The identification of the writer(s) of the *Odes of Solomon* is unknown.[11] What is known with certainty is that King Solomon lived

---

[9] Henry Constable, *The Duration and Nature of Future Punishment*, London: Hobbs and Hammond, 1886, 168.

[10] Froom, *op. cit.*, 767.

[11] General biographical and dating information is drawn from James H. Charlesworth, (ed.), *The Old Testament Pseudepigrapha*, Volume Two, New York: Doubleday, 1985.

and reigned during the tenth century BC and the odes, which date to no earlier than the late first century, were not written by him. The work is therefore properly classified as a pseudepigraphon.

Scholars have long debated the identification of the group responsible for producing the odes. Judaism, Christianity, and Gnosticism have all been proposed as potential sources. Since the odes do not mention the Temple or the Mosaic Law, they do not appear to be of Jewish origin. They speak of a Messianic figure, but in terms not typical of Orthodox Christianity. Since they don't fit neatly into either Judaism or Orthodox Christianity, perhaps they derived from a Gnostic source?

Prior to the discovery of English scholar J. Rendell Harris (see discussion below), *Ode* 1 was known from a Gnostic text written in Coptic. In *Ode* 8:14 and *Ode* 19:1–5, God is represented in rather untypical Jewish-Christian phraseology as having breasts. When milked by the Holy Spirit, believers are nurtured with salvific milk (the Son). Some have concluded from these circumstances that the odes are Gnostic in origin. However, the general consensus of scholars is that the true origin is most probably to be found in early Jewish Christianity.

The exact date of the composition is unknown. Estimates of dates range from late in the first century (by those scholars believing that the composition is from the very early Jewish-Christian church) to as late as the third century (by those who believe the composition is Gnostic in origin). Many scholars recognize a possible influence from Jewish apocalyptic thought, and concepts similar to those expressed in the Dead Sea Scrolls are found in the odes. If this influence does in fact exist, then a composition date near AD 100 would be likely.

It is reasonable to conclude that the work was most likely composed in the first half of the second century. If this conclusion is correct, then the Odes of Solomon[12] falls within the desired time period (AD 95–325) targeted in this book for evaluation of the view presented therein on the issue of human immortality.

The odes were virtually lost to mankind until discovered by J. Rendel Harris in 1909 in some old Syriac documents that he had procured sometime earlier during a trip to the Middle East. The manuscript in his possession was lacking the opening leaves and, of the forty-two odes, *Ode* 1 was missing in part and *Ode* 2 altogether. Previous to Harris's discovery, the odes were known only through notations in lists of apocryphal books, excerpts in the Coptic *Pistis Sophia*, and from a Latin quotation of *Ode* 19 by Lactantius in the fourth century. Perhaps it bears repeating that *Ode* 1 is known from a Gnostic source. *Ode* 2 has never been located.

Why were the *Odes of Solomon* written? They are poetic in form and bear a striking resemblance to the Psalms contained in the Jewish and Christian canons. The odes quote neither from the Old Testament nor from the New Testament. Charlesworth maintains that the writer was influenced by the former and by the traditions of the latter. He sees a major dependence on the Davidic Psalms and believes there is sufficient evidence to support the assumption that the writer(s) knew them both in Hebrew and Greek. He concludes that the *Odes of Solomon* is the earliest known Christian hymnbook.

In my review of Charlesworth's English translation of the odes, I found references bearing on the issue of human immortality in twenty-three of the extant forty-two odes. I shall briefly examine each of these passages in turn and propose a conclusion on the view on human immortality presented therein.

Ode 3:8 reads, "Indeed he who is joined to Him who is immortal, truly shall be immortal." The "Him" in this passage refers to God.

---

[12] Additional information can be found at: Early Christian Writings: New Testament, Apocrypha, Gnostics, Church Fathers, *Odes of Solomon*, www.earlychristianwritings.com/odes.html.

Those who are joined to the Immortal One shall be immortal. This suggests that those who are not joined to God shall not be immortal.

Ode 5:14 reads, "And though all things visible should perish, I shall not die." It is not clear at this point in the ode whether the writer is claiming that he already possesses immortality, and therefore cannot die, or if he is hinting at a future resurrection to immortality. However, we should note that this verse equates "perish" with "death."

Ode 6:15 reads, "Even living persons who were about to expire, they have held back from death." In this verse we find an equating of "expire" with "death." Those who still draw breath, though feebly, are held back from losing what is left of their breath and passing from the state of living to the state of death.

Ode 7:24 reads, "And let there not be anyone who breathes that is without knowledge or voice." This is an admonition for all who breathe (that is, for all who are alive) to acquire knowledge of God and speak boldly and joyfully of their knowledge. Those without breath are dead and have no ability to speak.

Ode 8:21-22 reads, "And you who were loved in the Beloved, and you who are kept in Him who lives, and you who are saved in Him who was saved. And you shall be found incorrupt in all ages, on account of the name of your Father." The "Beloved" refers to the unnamed Messiah. The Messiah himself is said to be saved and those found in him are saved. This at the very least implies that those not found in Messiah are not saved.

Ode 9:4 reads, "For in the will of the Lord is your life, and His purpose is eternal life, and your perfection is incorruptible." This verse associates the life of the believer with the purpose of God—that is, eternal life. This perfection is said to be "incorruptible." Presumably, one who is not a believer may anticipate that his/her status before God is imperfect and therefore will be found "corruptible."

Ode 9:7 reads, "And also that those who have known Him may not perish, and so that those who received Him may not be ashamed." This verse equates "knowing God" with the prospect (or hope?) of not "perishing." It further suggests a link between "perish" and "shame." Those who know God will not be ashamed. Those who have not known Him will be ashamed.

Ode 10:2 reads, "And He has caused to dwell in me His immortal life, and permitted me to proclaim the fruit of His peace." Here we see that God causes immortal life to dwell in the believer. The converse is implied for those who do not believe. That is, God will not cause immortal life to dwell in the unbeliever.

Ode 11:12 reads, "And from above He gave me immortal rest, and I became like the land that blossoms and rejoices in its fruits." This passage speaks of God giving the believer immortal rest. Immortality is thus presented as something that is given, rather than something that one already possesses.

Ode 15:8–10 reads, "I put on immortality through His name, and took off corruption by His grace. Death has been destroyed before my face, and Sheol has been vanquished by my word. And eternal life has arisen in the Lord's land, and it has been declared to His faithful ones, and has been given without limit to all that trust in Him." This verse is speaking about the Messiah putting on immortality. One does not put on something which one already possesses. Immortality is contrasted with corruption. Death, which is said to be destroyed by Messiah putting on immortality, is destroyed by this act. Death is also associated in this passage with Sheol, i.e. the place of the dead. The clothing of Messiah introduces eternal life in God's land. This suggests that, prior to this act, eternal life was not seen in God's land. If there was no eternal life found in the land prior to this event, then the opposite state, i.e. mortal life, is all that existed in the land.

Ode 22:8–10 reads, "And It chose them from the graves, and separated them from the dead ones. It took dead bones and covered them with flesh. But they were motionless, so It gave them energy for life." Here the word "It" refers to the right hand of God, i.e. the Messiah. It is the Messiah who chooses (rescues?) believers from their graves. This choosing separates the chosen from those who are not chosen. The ones who are not chosen remain behind in the grave. They are in a state of death. Messiah is said to take "dead bones," not "live bones," and cover them with flesh. Those who are so clothed with flesh are motionless until Messiah gives them energy (spirit?) for life, that is, reanimates them. (This sounds very much like a description of resurrection from death to life. This observation may not seem significant but it will be seen to be when compared with Charlesworth's view, which will be given below.) In contrast, those who are not chosen are not clothed with flesh, their bones remain dead, and they are not given energy to become reanimated.

Ode 23:20 reads, "Then all the seducers became headstrong and fled, and the persecutors became extinct and were blotted out." The "seducers" are those who have been seduced into unbelief and go about seducing others to unbelief. They flee away from, rather than running to, the source that is able to save them from death. They are said to become "extinct" and "blotted out." This means that they will die and the very remembrance of them will be removed.

Ode 24:9 reads, "And all of them who were lacking perished, because they were not able to express the word so that they might remain." Those who are lacking (in knowledge and belief) will perish. As we have observed previously, the writer equates "perish" with "death." These persons are not able to express the word, i.e. the confession of faith in Messiah. Is that inability due to their lack of knowledge/faith, or is it their inability to speak because they have died? Both understandings are possible.

Ode 26:11 reads, "Who can interpret the wonders of the Lord? Though he who interprets will be destroyed, yet that which was interpreted will remain." This is a difficult text, but it appears to be saying that although he who interprets God's acts is destroyed in death, the interpretation itself cannot be destroyed. This appears to me to be a reflection on the mortality of even those who are righteous. In other words, all human beings, whether righteous or wicked, will be destroyed in death. As we have seen in other passages, this destruction is not final for the righteous believer, though it is for the wicked unbeliever.

Ode 28:6–8 reads, "Because I am ready before destruction comes, and have been set on His immortal side. And immortal life embraced me, and kissed me. And from that life is the Spirit which is within me. And it cannot die because it is life." This verse seems to be an echo of *Ode* 26:11. The righteous man prepares himself for the destruction that all men must endure. He is confident that he has already been assured through his faith in Messiah that he will not remain in a state of destruction. His faith places him on the side of the one who is immortal and who has the ability to grant him immortality. Because of his faith, he is embraced (or has the sure hope of being embraced) by immortality. Conversely, those lacking this faith can hold no such sure hope. The writer goes on to link immortal life with the Spirit that is within, or will be in him again when his dead bones are clothed again with flesh and energized to become capable of motion. His immortality depends on the immortality of the energizing Spirit.

Ode 28:17 reads, "And I did not perish, because I was not their brother, nor was my birth like theirs." The speaker in this verse is apparently the Messiah. He is not denying that he died. He is claiming that he has been rescued from the grave while his enemies either have not been (or will not be) so rescued.

Ode 29:4 reads, "And he caused me to ascend from the depths of Sheol, and from the mouth of death He drew me." The "he" in this verse refers to the Messiah. The writer is saying that the Messiah has caused him to come out of the grave. This appears to be another example of resurrection of the believer from the grave. The writer equates "Sheol" with "the mouth of death."

Ode 29:10 reads, "And the Lord overthrew my enemy by His Word, and he became like the dust which a breeze carries off." The writer's enemy, the unbeliever, becomes like dust that is carried off in the wind. This sounds very much like the reduction of a person to ashes (in the lake of fire?) and the dissolution, or scattering, of the once united components of the body. This carries the connotation of utter destruction of the unbeliever.

Ode 31:7 reads, "And possess yourselves through grace, and take unto you immortal life." Immortal life is something that the writer urges his reader to take unto themselves. There is no need to urge people to take unto themselves something they already possess.

Ode 33:9 reads, "Be not corrupted nor perish." In this passage we find a parallel between "corrupted" and "perish." The writer is admonishing his readers to avoid this terrible end.

Ode 33:12 reads, "And they who have put me on shall not be falsely accused, but they shall possess incorruption in the new world." The "me" in this verse is Grace personified. Those who accept God's grace will possess incorruption in the age to come. This suggests that those who do not accept God's grace will not possess incorruption in that future day.

Ode 34:6 reads, "Grace has been revealed for your salvation. Believe and live and be saved." Salvation (from the penalty of sin, death) is found only through accepting the grace of God. Those who believe and live a righteous life will be saved. In contrast, those who do not accept God's grace are unbelievers. They will not live righteously and will not see salvation.

Ode 38:3 reads, "And became for me a haven of salvation, and set me on the place of immortal life." In context, it is Truth personified that sets the believer on the place of immortal life. Those who are not guided by Truth are not set on the place of immortal life. They remain set on the place of mortal life.

Ode 39:12 reads, "And they are neither blotted out, nor destroyed." This verse is speaking of the sure path of Messiah's footsteps. Just as his footsteps are not "blotted out, nor destroyed," neither will the footsteps of those who follow in Messiah's path—who place their trust in him. Those who do not obediently follow the Messiah walk a different path. There is no such assurance of protection from being "blotted out, nor destroyed" for those walking another path.

Ode 40:6 reads, "And His possessions are immortal life, and those who receive it are incorruptible." God's possession is immortal life. It is something that belongs to Him and man must receive it as a gift from Him in order to be incorruptible. If man possessed immortal life inherently, there would be no need to receive the gift of immortality from Him. Those who do not receive the gift are corruptible.

Ode 41:3 reads, "We live in the Lord by His grace, and life we receive by His Messiah." The "life" we receive by God's Messiah is that of immortality. There is no immortality for man apart from accepting the grace of God. That immortal life is dispensed by God's Messiah. Those who do not follow the Messiah do not receive life in the age to come.

Ode 41:11 reads, "And His Word is with us in all our way, the Savior who gives life and does not reject ourselves." God's "Word," the "Savior," is His Messiah. He gives (immortal) life to those who follow him. Those who do not follow the Messiah will be rejected. In other words, those who will not follow the Messiah will not receive (immortal) life from him.

Ode 41:15 reads, "The Messiah in truth is one. And He was known before the foundations of the world, that He might give life to persons for ever by the truth of His name." This verse restricts the gift of life to persons who accept the truth that the person able to give the gift is God's Messiah. Since all persons have life, the "gift of life" implies that Messiah is able in the name of his God, by His authority, to grant something that man lacks in his life. That something is immortality, but only for those who believe and follow him.

Ode 42:10–13 reads, "I was not rejected although I was considered to be so, and I did not perish although they thought it of me. Sheol saw me and was shattered, and Death ejected me and many with me. I have been vinegar and bitterness to it, and I went down with it as far as its depth. Then the feet and the head it released, because it was not able to endure my face." The speaker in this passage is the Messiah. His enemies thought they had caused him to perish. Ultimately, they have not. The place of the dead (the grave) and death were not able to hold him. This vivid imagery describes the resurrection of the Messiah from the dead. As we have seen in earlier passages, the hope of mortal man is to be resurrected from the dead, by the one who defeated death and the grave.

Without question, the author(s) of the *Odes of Solomon* presented a view on human immortality that is clearly Conditionalist in tenor. The description of dead bones being clothed with flesh and being reanimated by the injection of spirit is the classic description of resurrection from the dead. The author is blunt in confining this life to those who believe and follow Messiah.

Immortality is the possession of God alone. He granted it to His Messiah when He resurrected him from the place of the dead. The once mortal Messiah has put on immortality. It is this same Messiah who will resurrect from the place of the dead those who follow and obey him, and clothe them with immortality.

Charlesworth's comments on the concept of immortal life pictured in the odes are somewhat perplexing. He writes, "The Odist professes neither the Greek concept of an immortal soul that is transmigrated from one body to another nor the Jewish concept of the resurrection of the body.... The Odist rather exults in his salvation and experience of immortality because he has taken off a corrupt garment and put on a garment of incorruption.... All of this language is used to state emphatically that his immortality is geographically here and chronologically now."[13]

Certainly the odes do not profess the Greek concept of an immortal soul, even without speaking of transmigration "from one body to another." However, the odes do not fail to express the Jewish concept of the resurrection of the body.

Charlesworth understands the odist to say that the change from corruption to incorruption has literally occurred in the odist's natural lifetime—it is something that has already been obtained by the followers of Messiah. But it seems clear that the odist is expressing the sure hope that the follower has in Messiah. It is hope held in prospect; the literal accomplishment is sure but reserved for the day when the Messiah bodily resurrects the believer from the dead and clothes him with immortality.

I acknowledge both that I lack Charlesworth's academic credentials and that my understanding of the odes may be biased by my own belief in the Jewish concept of human immortality. It is possible that I am reading something into the text that is not there. Keeping that concession in mind, I am respectfully suggesting for consideration the proposition that the odist does in fact express the Jewish concept of a bodily resurrection of mortal believers to immortal life in the age to come.

Ignatius of Antioch

Ignatius Theophorus (this nickname means "the Bearer of God") was born approximately AD 35, probably in Syria. He was a pupil of Apostle John, and served as the third Bishop of Antioch at the end of the first century and the beginning of the second. He was martyred at

---

[13] Charlesworth, *op. cit.*, 731.

the Colosseum in Rome on Monday, December 20, AD 107, by being thrown to the lions.[14]

During his final journey (to Rome), Ignatius wrote seven epistles, usually referred to as *Ig. Ephesians*, *Ig. Magnesians, Ig. Trallians, Ig. Romans*, *Ig. Philadelphians*, *Ig. Smyrnaeans*, and *Ig. Polycar.*

These epistles contain many references to immortality and the final destiny of the unsaved. For example:

Ig. Ephesians 5:7 quotes *John* 3:36 as saying, "He who does not obey the Son shall **not see life**" (this is a substantially accurate quotation, except that Ignatius substitutes "obey" for John's "believe"). The point is that the unsaved will not experience "**life**" after their judgment.

Ig. Ephesians 7:1 describes the final destiny of those who "practice things unworthy of God" as "**destruction**" (not torment!), and the following verse (7:2) quotes *Proverbs* 11:3 as saying, "The **destruction** of the ungodly is sudden" (actually, *Proverbs* 11:3 says, "The perverseness of transgressors shall destroy them"—not exactly the same statement, but a similar statement using the same key word, "**destroy**"). Later in the same chapter (7:5–7), Ignatius says that "Jesus … was … **immortal**" though living "in a **mortal** body" and that "He became subject to corruption (i.e., the disintegration of the body that follows death), that He might free our **souls** from **death** and corruption, and heal (or, "save") them, and might restore them to health, when they were diseased with ungodliness and wicked lusts." If our "souls" must be freed from "death," they certainly cannot be "immortal" as Ignatius says Jesus was (i.e., before He "became subject to corruption")!

Ig. Ephesians 16:3, describing the fate of false teachers, says that "Those that corrupt mere human families are condemned to **death**"

---

[14] Lake, *op. cit.*, 166.

and that those "who endeavor to corrupt the Church" will "suffer **everlasting punishment**" precisely because Jesus, for the sake of the Church, "endured the cross, and submitted to **death**!" Apparently Ignatius saw "death" and "everlasting punishment" as essentially the same thing. In the next verse (16:4), he goes on to say that whoever "sets at nought His (i.e., Christ's) doctrine, shall go into **hell**"—and in the following verse (16:5), that "**In like manner**, every one that has received from God the power of distinguishing, and yet follows an unskillful shepherd (i.e., a false teacher), and receives a false opinion for the truth, shall **be punished**." Again, he seems to equate the "punishment" with "hell," which, in the previous verse, he had equated with "death." For Ignatius, then, the terms "death," "hell," and "everlasting punishment" would seem to be interchangeable, and all of them the literal opposite of "immortality."

Ig. Ephesians 17:1 says, "For this end did the Lord receive ointment on his head that he might **breathe immortality** on the Church."[15] (without such a "breathing," therefore, no human being would **possess** "immortality").

Ig. Ephesians 20:2 refers to the bread of Holy Communion as "the medicine of **immortality**, and the antidote which prevents us from **dying**, [which causes] that we should **live forever** in Jesus Christ." Again, Ignatius contrasts "immortality" and living "forever" with "dying" (not "undergoing eternal torment"!).

Ig. Magnesians 5:1 says, "Seeing, then, that **all** things (including, as we will see momentarily, human lives) have an **end**, and there is set before us **life** (meaning, of course, "eternal" life) upon our observance [of God's precepts], but **death** (not "eternal torment"!) as the result of disobedience,... let us flee from death, and make choice of life."

---

[15] Lake, *op. cit.*, 191.

Ig. Magnesians 10:1 reads, "For were He to reward us according to our works, we would **cease to be**." (The Greek expression here translated "cease to be" is *ouketi esmen*.)

Ig. Trallians 2:1 says, "For when you are in subjection to the bishop as to Jesus Christ it is clear to me that you are living not after men, but after Jesus Christ, who died for our sake, that by believing on his death you may escape **death** (not 'torment')."[16]

Ig. Trallians 8:3, referring to Jesus, says, "He gave Himself a ransom for us, that He might cleanse us by His blood from our old ungodliness, and **bestow life** on us when we were almost on the point of **perishing** through the depravity that was in us."

Ig. Trallians 11:3, referring to certain false teachers, says, "The children of the evil one ... produce **death**-bearing fruit (i.e., their false teaching), whereof if any one tastes, he instantly **dies**, and that not a mere temporary death, but one that shall endure for ever." (Notice that Ignatius says that their "**death**" shall "endure for ever," **not** their "souls"!)

By contrast to those who fall victim to the false teachers, *Ig. Trallians* 11:8 says, "Christ invites **you** to [share in] His immortality, by His passion and resurrection, inasmuch as ye are His members." So, according to Ignatius, the "members" of the Body of Christ (i.e. Christians) are invited to experience immortality **in contrast** to the victims of false teachers, who are threatened with a "**death**" that shall "endure for ever."

In *Ig. Romans* 4:2, Ignatius says, in regard to his approaching martyrdom, "Rather entice the wild beasts that they may become my tomb, and leave no trace of my body, that when I **fall asleep** I be not

---

16   *Ibid.*, 213–214.

burdensome to any."[17] Note that he says, "fall asleep," not "go to Heaven."

In Ig. Philadelphians 3:1, in a discussion of those who follow false teachers, Ignatius refers to the Devil (who "sponsors" false teachers) as "the destroyer of men"; a few verses later, in Ig. Philadelphians 3:7–10, he states that, "If any man does not stand aloof from the preacher of falsehood, he shall be condemned to hell.... Have no fellowship with such a man, lest you perish along with him, even should he be your father, your son, your brother, or a member of your family." Note that in this chapter Ignatius defines "condemnation to hell" as "destruction" and "perishing," not as "torment."

Ig. Philadelphians 8:6 refers to "Jesus Christ, to disobey whom is manifest destruction." (Again, not "torment.")

Ig. Smyrnaeans 6:1–2 boldly states, "Let no man deceive himself. Unless he believes that Christ Jesus has lived in the flesh, and shall confess His cross and passion, and the blood which He shed for the salvation of the world, he **shall not obtain eternal life**, whether he be a king, or a priest, or a ruler, or a private person, a master or a servant, a man or a woman." (If "eternal life" must be "obtained"—and there is a possibility that one might "**not obtain**" it, then it is clearly not something everyone inherently possesses.) Later in the same chapter (in *Ig. Smyrnaeans* 6:7), Ignatius quotes *John* 17:3 as saying, "This is life eternal, to know the only true God, and Jesus Christ whom He has sent." This is a substantially accurate quotation—the only change from the original being that Jesus spoke **to** God, in the second person, while Ignatius alters the quotation to the third person form—and, incidentally, this verse is yet another "favorite" of many modern Conditionalists, who use it to demonstrate that those who do not "know" God do not possess "life eternal."

---

[17] Lake, *op. cit.*, 231.

And in *Ig. Polycarp* 2:8, he admonishes his fellow bishop, "Be sober as God's athlete. The prize is immortality and eternal life, of which you have been persuaded."[18] If "immortality and eternal life" is a "prize," then it is obviously not something all human beings naturally possess!

In all his epistles, Ignatius "is utterly silent in regard to any Innate Immortality of the soul or anything akin thereto."[19] I conclude, therefore, that he must be classified as a Conditionalist.

Polycarp of Smyrna

Polycarp was born approximately AD 69 in Smyrna. He was a pupil of Apostle John, and as a young man "was brought into contact with many who had seen Christ" in person. He served as bishop of Smyrna during the first half of the second century. A letter from the church at Smyrna to the church in Philomelium, commonly known as *The Martyrdom of Polycarp*, preserves in meticulous detail the story of how Polycarp was burned at the stake in Smyrna on Saturday, February 23, AD 155, for refusing to give up his faith in Jesus.[20] The letter records his famous statement, "Eighty and six years have I served Him, and He never did me any injury: how then can I blaspheme my King and my Savior?"

According to Irenaeus of Lyons (AD 130–202), Polycarp wrote several epistles, but only one is available today—his *Epistle to the Philippians*, written around AD 109 as a "cover letter" for a collection of the writings of Ignatius of Antioch that Polycarp was sending to the church at Philippi. This epistle is commonly referred to as *Poly. Philippians*.

---

[18] *Ibid.*, 271.
[19] Froom, *op. cit.*, 773.
[20] Lake, *op. cit.*, 280.

Poly. Philippians does not contain many direct references to immortality and the final destiny of unbelievers, but there are several indirect references to this topic:

Poly. Philippians 2:2 says, "Now, 'he who raised him' (i.e., Jesus) from the dead 'will also raise us up' **if** we do his will, and walk in his commandments and love the things which he loved, refraining from all unrighteousness, covetousness, love of money, evil speaking, false witness, 'rendering not evil for evil, or railing for railing,' or blow for blow, or curse for curse"[21] (implying that he will **not** "raise us up" if we **don't** do his will).

Poly. Philippians 5:2 similarly states, "Likewise must the deacons be blameless before his righteousness, as the servants of God and Christ and not of man, not slanderers, not double-tongued, not lovers of money, temperate in all things, compassionate, careful, walking according to the truth of the Lord, who was the 'servant of all.' For **if** we please him in this present world we shall receive from him that which is to come; even as he promised to raise us from the dead, and that **if** we are worthy citizens of his community, 'we shall also reign with him,' **if** we have but faith."[22] Notice again the threefold repetition of the "conditionalist" word **if**, indicating that we shall **not** "receive from him that which is to come," he will **not** "raise us from the dead," and we shall **not** "reign with him" if we **do not** "please him," **do not** be "worthy citizens of his community," and **do not** have faith.

Poly. Philippians 7:1 says that "Whosoever perverts the oracles of the Lord to his own lusts, and says that there is neither a resurrection nor a judgment, he is the first-born of Satan."

Poly. Philippians 9:1–2 says that "Ignatius, and Zosimus, and Rufus ... and ... Paul himself, and the rest of the apostles ... are [gone] into their deserved place beside the Lord...." This passage says

---

[21] *Ibid.*, 285.
[22] Lake, *op. cit.*, 289.

nothing at all about the fate of unbelievers, which is the question at issue between Conditionalists and Naturalists. Also, note that the word "gone" is printed in brackets, indicating that the translator supplied it on the theory that it is "implied" in the Greek text, though it is **not** actually **included** in it. Finally, note that Polycarp says these deceased apostles "are [gone] into their deserved place beside the Lord..."—**not** that they are "in Heaven" (since the Lord is known to be omnipresent, this isn't really saying a whole lot).

The Martyrdom of Polycarp also contains several references to these topics, some of which are purported to be quotations from Polycarp himself, as, for example, the following:

"You (referring to the proconsul) threaten me with fire which burns for an hour, and after a little is extinguished, but [you] are ignorant of the fire of the coming judgment..., reserved for the ungodly." (*Martyrdom* 11:4)

"I give You (referring to God) thanks that You have counted me worthy of this day and this hour, that I should have a part in ... the resurrection ... both of soul and body..." (*Martyrdom* 14:3).

(Other references to immortality in *The Martyrdom of Polycarp* should be studied separately, as not necessarily reflecting Polycarp's own views, but the views of the authors of the letter. I have not included these authors as "sources" for this book, since it is uncertain how much of the present text of the letter is original, and how much reflects interpolation by later copyists, several of whom are listed in the present text of Chapter 22.)

Polycarp may not have specifically stated that he believed in the final destruction of those who reject Christ, but at least "he never intimates the endless existence of the lost in eternal suffering."[23]

---

[23] Froom, *op. cit.*, 796.

Barring much evidence to the contrary, then, I feel I must classify him, along with his good friend, Ignatius, as a Conditionalist.

Papias of Hierapolis

Papias was born approximately AD 70; we do not know where. He was a pupil of Apostle John, a friend of "others who had seen the Lord," and of Polycarp of Smyrna, and served as bishop of Hierapolis, in Phrygia, during the first half of the second century.[24] He was martyred in Pergamus around AD 163.[25]

Papias wrote a five-volume book titled *Explanation of the Lord's Discourses* which was frequently quoted by later writers such as Irenaeus of Lyons (AD 130–202) and Eusebius of Caesarea (AD 263–339). Since no copies of this book have survived to the present day, we know of its contents only from fragments preserved in these quotations.

In none of these fragments does Papias deal directly with the question of human immortality, but there is one passage in which he quotes *1 Corinthians* 15:25–26, where Apostle Paul states, "For he (Jesus) must reign, till he (God) hath put all enemies under his (Jesus') feet. The last enemy that shall be destroyed is death." This is a "favorite" passage for many Conditionalists who understand it as teaching that, first, unbelievers will be "destroyed," then, the destroying agent ("death") will itself cease to exist. The Naturalist writers I have consulted seldom refer to this passage at all. It would be difficult, on such slim evidence, to draw a conclusion as to what position Papias held, except to say that, if he were a Naturalist, he didn't leave any clues behind (that we know of) to convince us that he

---

[24] Elgin Moyer, *Wycliffe Biographical Dictionary of the Church*, Chicago: Moody Press, 1982, 314.

[25] Alexander Roberts, *The Ante-Nicene Fathers*, New York: Charles Scribner's Sons, 1903, vol. 1, 151.

was. I therefore prefer to classify him, along with his good friend, Polycarp of Smyrna, as a Conditionalist.

The Writer(s) of the *Didache*

The *Didache*, or *Teaching of the Twelve Apostles*, is a catechetical handbook (a manual to be used in instructing new converts to Christianity) written around AD 120 in either Egypt or Syria.[26] It presents the moral standards of Christianity as the "Way of Life" (*Didache* 1:2) and sin as the "Way of Death" (*Didache* 5:1).

So far from implying that this "death" involves endless torment of immortal souls, this earliest known attempt at "Systematic Theology" implies that unbelievers will not even so much as rise for judgment! *Didache* 16:6–7 says, "And 'then shall appear the signs' of the truth. First the sign spread out in Heaven, then the sign of the sound of the trumpet, and thirdly the resurrection of the dead: **but not of all the dead**, but as it was said, 'The Lord shall come and all his saints with him.'"[27]

This position (the nonresurrection of the wicked dead) has, in modern times, been held by a small minority of Conditionalists—for example, by the Life and Advent Union denomination, which was founded in 1863, and merged with the Advent Christian General Conference of America in 1964—but it has certainly never been held by any Naturalists! There is little question, then, but that I must classify the writer(s) of the *Teaching of the Twelve Apostles* with the other Conditionalists of the early part of the second century.

This fact can be further illustrated by reference to *Didache* 10:2, which says, "We give thanks to You, O Holy Father, for Your Holy Name which You have made to tabernacle in our hearts, and for the

---

[26] Froom, *op. cit.*, 774–775.
[27] Lake, *op. cit.*, 333.

knowledge and faith and **immortality which You have made known to us through Jesus** Your Child."[28] This statement implies that the author(s) of the *Didache* **did not** believe that immortality was a natural attribute of the human soul or spirit. The next verse (*Didache* 10:3) says, "You, Lord Almighty, have created all things for Your Name's sake, and have given food and drink to men for their enjoyment, that they might give thanks to You, **but us have You blessed with** spiritual food and drink and **eternal light through Your Child** (Jesus)."[29] This statement, too, implies that the author(s) did not believe that the unsaved (referred to in the verse as "men") naturally possess eternal life (referred to in the verse as "eternal light").

I am, therefore, convinced that the unknown author(s) of the *Didache* was, or were, Conditionalist(s).

Quadratus of Athens

Quadratus was born toward the end of the first century, somewhere in Asia Minor. "According to Eusebius, he claimed to have been a disciple of the apostles."[30] He served as bishop of Athens during the first half of the second century. We do not know anything about the time or circumstances of his death.

AD 126, Quadratus wrote an *Apology for the Christian Religion* which was addressed to Emperor Hadrian. Only a small fragment of this work has been preserved.

What little we have of the *Apology* emphasizes the resurrection of the dead, frequently using such terms as "raised from the dead" and "raised up." It makes no mention whatever of the concept of an undying soul. Admittedly this evidence is scanty, but failing any other

---

[28] *Ibid.*, 324–325.
[29] *Ibid.*, 325.
[30] Moyer, *op. cit.*, 337.

evidence than this, I prefer to classify Quadratus, at least tentatively, as a Conditionalist, along with his friend and fellow-citizen, Aristides of Athens.

"Mathetes"

"Mathetes" (the word means "a disciple") was born sometime during the second half of the first century; we do not know where. He was "a disciple of the apostles" (according to his *Homily on the Word* 1:1).[31] We do not know anything about the time or circumstances of his death.

About AD 130, "Mathetes" wrote a *Homily on the Word*, the beginning chapter(s) of which are no longer known, but the last two chapters of which were preserved by the fact that an unknown copyist appended them to the *Epistle to Diognetus* (possibly the same Diognetus who was the tutor of the Roman Emperor, Marcus Aurelius), a copy of which was discovered AD 1592, then destroyed by a fire AD 1870. No one knows who had originally written that epistle (commonly referred to as *Diognetus*), nor when or where. The *Homily on the Word* is often presented as *Diognetus* 11:1–12:9; however, I will take the liberty of renumbering its verses as *Homily on the Word* 1:1–2:9.

Homily on the Word 2:2 says that "It is not the tree of knowledge that **destroys**—it is disobedience that proves **destructive**." *Homily on the Word* 2:3–4 go on to say, "God ... planted the tree of life in the midst of paradise, revealing ... the way to life.... For neither can **life** exist without knowledge, nor is knowledge secure without **life**."

If "**life**" cannot exist without knowledge, then, clearly, human beings cannot be immortal by nature since, if they were, their lives

---

[31] Roberts, *op. cit.*, vol. 1, 23.

would continue to exist forever even if they did not acquire knowledge.

I feel justified, then, though perhaps with something less than certainty, in classifying "Mathetes" (tentatively, at least) as a Conditionalist.

Clement of Corinth

The document commonly called *2 Clement* has long been puzzling to patristic scholars. According to M. B. Riddle, it is the work of "an unknown author" who may have been the bishop of Corinth "between AD 120 and AD 140"[32]—for this reason, I will call him "Clement of Corinth" as a means of honoring both the tradition that it was written by "Clement" and the probability that it was written in Corinth.

2 Clement 1:7 states that Jesus Christ "saved us when we were ready to **perish**"; verse 9 of the same chapter adds that "Our whole life was nothing else than **death**"; and verse 11 refers to "the **destruction** to which we were exposed (before He saved us)."

2 Clement 2:6 describes "sinners" (*2 Clement* 2:5, quoting *Matthew* 9:13) as "those who are **perishing**"; *2 Clement* 2:8 also refers to them as **"perishing"** and "hastening to **destruction**."

By contrast, *2 Clement* 5:5 describes "the promise of Christ" as **"life everlasting**," and verse 6 goes on to ask, "By what course of conduct, then, shall we **attain** [this blessing]?" Of course, no "course of conduct" would be necessary to "obtain" something that one already possessed by nature!

In Chapter 6, Clement discusses the "enmity" between "this world and the next" (verse 4). In this context, he describes the things "which

---

[32] Roberts, *op. cit.*, vol. 7, 513.

are to come" as being "**incorruptible**" (verse 7). By contrast (if we do not "do the will of Christ"), "nothing shall deliver us from eternal punishment" (verse 8). Since the opposite of "incorruptible" is, by definition, "corruptible," Clement's view of "eternal punishment" must be that of "corruption" (a word often used interchangeably with both "death" and "destruction" in the writings we have been studying).

Again, *2 Clement* 7:3 refers to "the straight course" as "the race that is **incorruptible**" and *2 Clement* 7:7 refers to it as "the **incorruptible** contest."

In Chapter 8, Clement says that "by doing the will of the Father, and keeping the flesh holy, and observing the commandments of the Lord, we shall **obtain** eternal life" (verse 4) and actually "quotes" the Lord as saying, "Keep the flesh holy and the seal undefiled, that ye may **receive** eternal life" (verse 6). "Some have thought this a quotation from an unknown apocryphal book, but it seems rather an explanation of the preceding words."[33]

2 Clement 15:2 uses the rather rare expression "**perishing soul**" to describe an unsaved hearer of his message. In Chapter 17, he exhorts his hearers, "Let us therefore repent from the whole heart, that no one of us **perish**" (verse 1) and exclaims, "How much more ought a **soul** already knowing God not to **perish**!" (verse 2). Later in the same chapter, he says, "Let us attempt to make advances in the commandments of the Lord, that ... we may be gathered together unto **life** (clearly, eternal life)" (verse 4). By contrast, in verse 10, he says that "Those that have ... denied Jesus ... are punished with grievous torments in unquenchable fire." He does not, however (as modern Naturalists often do), insist that these "torments" continue forever. Saying that the "fire" is "unquenchable" merely emphasizes that its destructive work will continue unabated until it is completed! Remember, this fate is positioned to be opposite to the promise of (eternal) "**life**" to those who escape it. It cannot consist, then, in

---

[33] *Ibid.*, 519, footnote 16.

"living forever" in a "worse condition." It must consist of eventually **ceasing** to live.

In Chapter 19, Clement urges his hearers to "repent with the whole heart, thus **giving** to yourselves salvation and [eternal] **life**" (verse 2). Later in the same chapter, he promises those who "suffer evil in the world" that "they shall enjoy the **immortal** fruit of the **resurrection**" (verse 8), leading to the experience of "**living** again ... for an eternity" (verse 10).

Finally, in his concluding doxology, Clement refers to Jesus as the "Prince of **incorruption**" (*2 Clement* 20:6).

Clement's book (which is really a homily, or sermon) acquired the title "*2 Clement*" because for a long time it was mistakenly thought (by many people) to have been written by Clement of Rome, whose *Epistle to the Corinthians* (the only work he is known to have written) was therefore called "*1 Clement*" (see above). Certainly this mistake could not have been made had Clement of Corinth held to a different view of such a foundational doctrine as that of Human Immortality. But we have already seen that there is no doubt but that Clement of Rome was a Conditionalist. This fact alone—bolstered, however, as it is, by the numerous references just cited—is sufficient to make it clear that Clement of Corinth, like his predecessor and namesake, was a Conditionalist.

Barnabas of Alexandria

The so-called *Epistle of Barnabas* was written approximately AD 135 by an unknown Jewish Christian who is now commonly referred to as "Barnabas of Alexandria." This Barnabas is not Apostle Barnabas who accompanied Apostle Paul, but he is usually classified as one of the Apostolic Fathers.[34]

---

[34] Froom, *op. cit.*, 778.

In several places Barnabas describes the reward of the Christian as an opportunity to "live forever" (thus implying that the unsaved will **not** live forever). For example:

In *Barnabas* 6:3, he quotes *Isaiah* 28:16 as saying, "He who hopes in him shall live forever." Actually, *Isaiah* 28:16 reads, "He that believeth shall not make haste." Apostle Paul similarly rephrases this verse when he quotes it, in *Romans* 10:11, as saying, "Whosoever believeth on him shall not be ashamed."[35] In any case, Barnabas' point (by implication) is that those who do **not** "hope in him" will **not** "live forever."

In *Barnabas* 8:5, he refers to this quote again, saying, "And why was the wool put on the wood? Because the kingdom of Jesus is on the wood, and because those who hope on him shall live forever."[36]

In *Barnabas* 9:6, he quotes *Psalm* 34:12 as asking, "Who is he that wishes to live forever?" Actually, *Psalm* 34:12 reads, "What man is he that desireth life, and loveth many days?" So, while David may only have been asking about a long life, Barnabas clearly understands him to be asking about eternal life. But, if human beings naturally possessed immortality, neither question would make any sense.

In *Barnabas* 11:10, he refers to *Ezekiel* 47:1–12 as teaching that "There was a river flowing on the right hand, and beautiful trees grew out of it, and whoever shall eat of them shall live forever."[37] This is a fair summary of the rather lengthy passage in *Ezekiel*. *Barnabas* 11:11 goes on to "explain" this teaching by saying, "He means that whoever hears and believes these things spoken shall live forever."[38]

---

[35] Lake, *op. cit.*, 359.
[36] *Ibid.*, 369–371.
[37] *Ibid.*, 383.
[38] Lake, *op. cit.*, 383.

Regarding the destiny of unbelievers, *Barnabas* 6:2 quotes *Isaiah* 50:9 as saying, "Woe unto you, for you shall all wax old as a garment and the moth shall eat you up."[39] This is a fairly accurate quotation.

In *Barnabas* 11:7, he quotes *Psalm* 1:4–6 as saying, "It is not so with the wicked, it is not so; but they are even as the chaff which the wind drives away from the face of the earth. Therefore **the wicked shall not rise up** in judgment, nor sinners in the counsel of the righteous, for the Lord knows the way of the righteous, and the way of **the ungodly shall perish**."[40] This, too, is a fairly accurate quotation, and the passage is another "favorite" of many Conditionalist writers. Note that Barnabas has rephrased *Psalm* 1:5 slightly, so that it reads, "The wicked **shall not rise up** in judgment," where the Psalm actually says, "The wicked **shall not stand** in the judgment." This may be an indication that he held to the "nonresurrectionist" position I have described in connection with our discussion of the *Didache* (see above).

Barnabas 15:9 says, "His Son, coming [again], shall **destroy the time** of the wicked man, and judge the ungodly...." If the "time" of the wicked man is to be "destroyed" by the "judgment" of the "ungodly," the wicked and ungodly men must themselves be "destroyed," or they would somehow be existing without having any "time" in which to do so. Three verses later (15:12), Barnabas goes on to say, "We ourselves, having received the promise, **wickedness no longer existing**, and all things having been made new by the Lord, shall be able to work righteousness." If "wickedness" is no longer to be "existing" after the judgment day, then wicked, ungodly people must themselves no longer be existing then. So they certainly cannot be immortal if there is to come a time when they will cease to exist.

Barnabas 20:1 says that "The Way of the Black One (i.e., the Devil) is crooked and full of cursing, for it is the way of **death eternal**

---

39 *Ibid.*, 359.
40 *Ibid.*, 381.

with punishment, and in it are the things that **destroy their soul**: idolatry, frowardness, arrogance of power, hypocrisy, double-heartedness, adultery, murder, robbery, pride, transgression, fraud, malice, self-sufficiency, enchantments, magic, covetousness, the lack of the fear of God."[41]

And *Barnabas* 21:1–3 says, "It is good, therefore, that he who has learned the ordinances of the Lord, as many as have been written, should walk in them. For he who does these things shall be glorified in the kingdom of God, and **he who chooses the others shall perish** with his works. For this reason there is a resurrection, for this reason there is a recompense."[42]

In the entire epistle no mention is made of an "immortal soul" or of "endless torment." Clearly, Barnabas of Alexandria must be classified as a Conditionalist.

Aristides of Athens

Marcianus Aristides was born sometime late in the first century, probably in Athens. He was a philosopher, and continued to wear his philosopher's robe after he became a Christian in the early part of the second century. We do not know anything about the time or circumstances of his death.

Aristides wrote an *Apology* approximately AD 140, addressed to the Roman Emperor Antoninus. This book was lost for hundreds of years, but was rediscovered in the late nineteenth century.[43]

The *Apology* makes two statements on the subject of immortality. In Chapter 1, it says that "God" (not man!) is "immortal"; and, in

---

41 *Ibid.*, 407.
42 *Ibid.*, 407–409.
43 Moyer, *op. cit.*, 16.

Chapter 7, it says that man "has a beginning and an **end**" and is "**destroyed**" by "death." These affirmations are common in Conditionalist writings. On the other hand, Aristides does not make any statements that would incline me to the view that he was a Naturalist. Therefore, I classify him as a Conditionalist.

Hermas of Rome

Hermas was born approximately AD 100 in Rome. His brother, Pius I, served as the tenth Bishop of Rome AD 140–155.[44] Hermas and Pius may have been grandsons of the Hermas to whom Apostle Paul sent greetings in *Romans* 16:14. We do not know anything about the time or circumstances of his death.

About AD 154, Hermas wrote a novel (a sort of "second-century *Pilgrim's Progress*") called *The Pastor* (or *The Shepherd*), which is in three parts, known, respectively, as the *Visions*, the *Commandments*, and the *Similitudes* (or *Parables*). Pius officially commended this book "as a useful instruction for the people." As a result, it became very popular, and many people thought it should be included in the New Testament.

The Shepherd frequently uses the expression "live unto God" to mean "live forever" (a usage possibly derived from *Romans* 6:10, where Apostle Paul, speaking of Christ, says, "In that he died, he died unto sin once: but in that he lives, he **lives unto God**"—clearly, in this context, meaning, "He lives forever"), and almost always connects this expression with some condition such as "**if** you shall keep all these commandments." Here are some examples of this usage:

---

[44] Solomon Schepps, *The Lost Books of the Bible*, New York: Bell Publishing Company, 1979, 197, and Hoffman, *op. cit.*, 509.

"Keep these things, and cast all lust and iniquity far from you, and put on righteousness, and you shall live unto God, **if** you shall keep this commandment." (*Commandments* 1:5)

"And whoever shall hearken to this command, and do it, and shall depart from all lying, he shall live unto God." (*Commandments* 3:10)

"You shall live **if** you shall keep these my commandments. And whoever shall hear and do these commands shall live unto God." (*Commandments* 4:17)

"Keep therefore your chastity and modesty, and you shall live unto God." (*Commandments* 4:27)

"As many as shall repent with all their hearts, shall live unto God." (*Commandments* 5:9)

"Whoever shall observe these commandments shall live unto God." (*Commandments* 5:19)

"As many as shall submit to his work, shall live also unto God." (*Commandments* 6:18)

"Keep yourself therefore from them, that you may live unto God." (*Commandments* 8:7)

"**If** you shall keep all these commandments, you shall live unto God. And all those who shall keep these commandments shall live unto God." (*Commandments* 8:12)

"Do you therefore keep the virtue of faith, and depart from doubting, in which is no virtue, and you shall live unto God. And all shall live unto God, as many as do these things." (*Commandments* 9:11)

"Cleanse yourself from sadness, which is evil, and you shall live unto God. And all others shall live unto God, as many as shall lay aside sadness and put on cheerfulness." (*Commandments* 10:23)

"Whoever therefore shall depart from all evil desires, shall live unto God." (*Commandments* 12:6)

"Keep his commands, that you may live unto God." (*Commandments* 12:33)

"And all they also shall keep them who shall cleanse their hearts from the vain desires of the present world, and shall live unto God." (**Commandments** 12:36)

"**If** you do these things, and fear him, and abstain from every evil work, you shall live unto God." (*Similitudes* 5:6)

"Keep therefore both of them pure, and you shall live unto God." (*Similitudes* 5:63)
"Whoever shall walk in them shall live unto God." (*Similitudes* 6:1)

"Walk in my commands, and you shall live unto God." (*Similitudes* 6:6)

"Say unto all men that they repent, and they shall live unto God." (*Similitudes* 8:79)

"Whoever shall repent with all their hearts, and cleanse themselves from all the evils that I have before mentioned, and not add anything more to their sins, shall receive from the Lord the cure of their former iniquities, **if** they shall not make any doubt of these commands, and shall live unto God." (*Similitudes* 8:82)

"**If** these therefore shall repent, they shall live unto God." (*Similitudes* 9:204)

By contrast, in many places, Hermas describes the final destiny of the wicked as "death," "destruction," "not live," "die unto God," etc. Here are some examples of this usage:

"The remembrance of evils works **death**." (*Visions* 2:23)

"Be innocent and without disguise; so shall you be like an infant who knows no malice which **destroys the life** of man." (*Commandments* 2:1)

"They who do such things follow the way of **death**." (*Commandments* 4:2)

"The evil way has not a good end, but has many stumbling blocks; it is rugged and full of thorns, and leads to **destruction**." (*Commandments* 6:4)

"He that cannot keep himself from these things, cannot live unto God." (*Commandments* 8:4)

"It is very horrible and wild: and by its wildness **consumes** men. And especially if a servant of God shall chance to fall into it, except he be very wise, he is **ruined** by it. For it **destroys** those who have not the garment of a good desire: and are engaged in the affairs of the present world; and delivers them unto **death**." (*Commandments* 12:2)

"They that are subject unto [evil desires] shall **die forever**." (*Commandments* 12:6)

"Fear the Lord Almighty, who is able to save and to **destroy** you." (*Commandments* 12:33)

"The wicked, like the trees which you saw dry, shall as such be found dry and without fruit in that other world; and like dry wood shall be **burnt**." (*Similitudes* 4:4)

"If you shall defile the Holy Spirit, you shalt **not live**." (*Similitudes* 5:59)

"These kind of men are ordained to **death**." (*Similitudes* 6:13)

"They that are **dead**, are **utterly gone** forever." (*Similitudes* 6:15)

"Whoever shall continue in them, and shall not repent of what they have done, shall bring **death** upon themselves." (*Similitudes* 6:44)

"All these are dead unto God: and you see that none of them have repented, although they have heard my commands which you have delivered to them. From these men therefore **life is far distant**." (*Similitudes* 8:52)

"They that shall not repent shall lose both [the opportunity for] repentance and life." (*Similitudes* 8:54)

"For those who repent not, **death** is prepared." (*Similitudes* 8:55)

"They that shall not repent, but shall continue on in their wicked doings, shall **die the death**." (*Similitudes* 8:59)

"If anyone shall again return to his dissension, he shall be shut out from the tower, and shall **lose his life**." (*Similitudes* 8:63)

"By seditions and contempt of the law, they shall purchase **death** to themselves." (*Similitudes* 8:64)

"**If** they shall not repent, they shall **die**." (*Similitudes* 8:67)

"Many have altogether departed from God. These have **utterly lost life**." (*Similitudes* 8:68)

"If they shall continue in their evil doing they shall die." (Similitudes 8:69)

"They that repent not, but continue still in their pleasures, are nigh to death." (Similitudes 8:74)

"They that shall continue to add to their transgressions, and shall still converse with the lusts of the present world, shall condemn themselves to death." (Similitudes 8:83)

"If they shall live wickedly, they shall be doubly punished, and shall die forever." (Similitudes 9:173)

"If they shall continue in their evil courses, they shall be delivered to those women that will take away their life." (Similitudes 9:192)

"These also may live, if they shall presently repent; but if not, they shall be delivered to those women, who shall take away their life." (Similitudes 9:197)

"**If** you shall not [repent], you shall be delivered to him unto **death**." (*Similitudes* 9:209)
"But he who will repent must hasten on his repentance, before the building of this tower is finished: otherwise he shall be delivered by those women to **death**." (*Similitudes* 9:225)

"The words of such persons infect and **destroy** men." (*Similitudes* 9:227)

"Some of them, having repented, have been saved, and so shall others of the same kind be also saved, **if** they shall repent; but **if** not, they shall **die**." (*Similitudes* 9:228)

"Take heed therefore, you who have such thoughts, that this mind continue not in you, and you die unto God." (*Similitudes* 9:238)

"**If** you shall continue in malice, and in the remembrance of injuries, no such sinners shall live unto God." (*Similitudes* 9:276)

"But they that shall not keep his commands, **flee from their life**, and are adversaries to it. And they that follow not his commands, shall deliver themselves to **death**." (*Similitudes* 10:13)

"And whoever shall walk in these commands shall live, and be happy in his life. But he that shall neglect them, **shall not live**." (*Similitudes* 10:23)

The doctrine of Conditional Immortality has perhaps never been more clearly expressed than in *Commandments* 7:6, which reads, "They only who fear the Lord and keep His commandments have life with God; but as to those who keep not His commandments, there is no life in them."

"Hermas clearly does not hold to inherent, indefeasible immortality for the wicked."[45] At no point in this book (which is about as long, in verses, as the *Gospel According to Matthew*) does he mention, or even hint at, the concepts of the soul going to Heaven or Hell at death, the eternal torment of the damned, an "immortal soul," or an "undying spirit." Yet, so far from representing a minority position in the Early Church, we know that *The Shepherd* was **quoted as Scripture** by Irenaeus of Lyons (AD 130–202); was **praised** by Tertullian of Carthage (AD 145–220); was **considered divinely inspired** by Origen of Alexandria (AD 185–254); was **read publicly in the churches** in the time of Eusebius of Caesarea (AD 263–339); was **cited** by Athanasius of Alexandria (AD 296–373); was **applauded** by Jerome of Bethlehem (AD 345–420); and was **attached to some of the most ancient manuscripts of the New Testament itself!**[46] I must conclude both that Hermas himself was a Conditionalist and that he wrote *The Shepherd* at a time in history when Conditionalism was held by the predominant majority of Christians.

---

[45] Froom, *op. cit.*, 788.
[46] Schepps, *op. cit.*, 197.

Furthermore, since we have now completed our study of the Apostolic Fathers, and found none of them to be Naturalists, I must agree with Dr. James K. Brandyberry's conclusion that, "the teaching of innate immortality is absent from the Apostolic Fathers, those Christian writers who lived nearest to or whose lives partly paralleled the last of the apostles."[47]

The Subapostolic Fathers

As mentioned previously, the Subapostolic Fathers who wrote on the subject of human immortality were:

Justin of Samaria (AD 106–165)
Tatian of Assyria (AD 110–180)
Theophilus of Antioch (AD 115–181)
Melito of Sardis (AD ?–190)
Athenagoras of Athens (AD 127–190)
Polycrates of Ephesus (AD 125–196)
Irenaeus of Lyons (AD 130–202)

Their writings cover approximately the second half of the second century.

Justin of Samaria

Flavius Justinus, popularly known as Justin Martyr (this nickname means "the Witness"), was born approximately AD 106 in Flavia Neapolis (formerly known as Shechem, now known as Nablus), in Samaria. As a young man, he studied in all of the major philosophical schools of the Greeks—Stoic, Aristotelian, Pythagorean, and Platonist.

---

[47] James Brandyberry, *The Development of the Doctrine of Immortality from the Apostolic Fathers to Augustine, Henceforth*, Volume XII, Number 1, 1983, 4.

"These philosophies never satisfied him."[48] He was converted to Christianity around AD 130, but continued to wear the distinctive clothing of a philosopher, "as a token that he had attained the only true philosophy." He traveled extensively, eventually (by AD 150) settling in Rome, where he worked as a teacher. Justin "was really the first to strive to interpret Christianity from the Greek point of view." During this time, Christians were constantly being persecuted. Along with other Christians, Justin was interrogated by Q. Junius Rusticus, who was the prefect of the city of Rome. The Christians were ordered to renounce Christianity and offer sacrifices to the Roman gods. Along with Justin, they all refused to renounce their faith and were therefore beheaded for their profession of Christianity sometime in 166.

Justin's writings include his *First Apology* (AD 155), a *Dialogue with Trypho* (AD 158), and his *Second Apology* (AD 161), as well as several smaller and lesser-known treatises, such as *Discourse to the Greeks*, *Address to the Greeks*, *On the Sole Government of God*, and *On the Resurrection*.

In *First Apology* 8:2, Justin says, "Impelled by the **desire** of the eternal and pure life, we [Christians] **seek** the abode that is with God, the Father and Creator of all, and hasten to confess our faith, persuaded and convinced as we are that they who have proved to God by their works that they followed Him, and loved to abide with Him where there is no sin to cause disturbance, can **obtain** these things." Dustin Smith (in his unpublished paper on Justin Martyr) comments, "Eternal life … sounds like something that we do not have because it is something that we long for … eternal life is something that we can obtain."[49] But why would we **desire**—and why would we need to **obtain**—eternal life if we already possessed it by nature?

In *First Apology* 10:4, Justin says, "In the beginning [God] created us when we were not," and he goes on to argue, on this premise, "In

---

48 Dustin Smith, *Justin Martyr* (unpublished manuscript), 2006, 1.
49 Smith, *op. cit.*, 1–2.

like manner, those who choose what is pleasing to Him are ... deemed worthy of incorruption...." This argument would seem to imply that: 1) those who do not choose what is pleasing to Him are not deemed worthy of incorruption, or immortality; and 2) since the unsaved did not exist before being created, they will not exist when the saved are made immortal.

In *First Apology* 13:1, Justin presents one of several duties of a Christian as "to present before [God] petitions for our existing again in incorruption through faith in Him." If, however, souls (even of those who do not have faith in Him) are by nature incorruptible, as Plato had taught, why would such "petitions" need to be presented?

In *First Apology* 21:9, Justin says that "**Only** those who have lived near to God are **made immortal**." Clearly, from his use of the word "made" in this context, he means to imply that they are not "automatically" immortal; also, from his use of the word "only," he certainly implies that those who have **not** "lived near to God" are **not** immortal.

Similarly, in *Discourse to the Greeks* 5:6, Justin says, "The [Divine] Word ... **makes** mortals **immortal**...." It seems like overstating the obvious to point out that "mortals" (by definition) are **not** "immortal"—and that it takes the miraculous intervention of God to "make" them so! Yet such an obvious statement is precisely what those who hold to Naturalism deny.

In *First Apology* 26:2–4, as part of a lengthy section on false prophets, Justin describes the career and subsequent veneration of Simon Magus (see Acts 8:9–24), going on (in verse 5) to describe Meander of Capparetea as "a disciple of Simon [Magus], and inspired by devils...." In verse 6, he informs us that Meander "persuaded those who adhered to him **that they should never die**..."—thus, by implication, affirming, as he does elsewhere, that the wicked **do** eventually **die** (as opposed to living forever in conscious torment).

In *First Apology* 39:10, comparing the loyalty of Roman soldiers to the Roman emperor with the loyalty of Christians to Christ, Justin says, "If the soldiers enrolled by you, and who have taken the military oath, prefer their allegiance [to you] to their own life ... though you can **offer** them **nothing incorruptible**, it were verily ridiculous if **we**, who **earnestly long for incorruption**, should not endure all things (e.g. persecution, torture, death), in order to **obtain** what we desire (i.e., incorruption, or immortality) from Him (i.e., God) who is able to **grant** it." Why would Christians "earnestly long" to "obtain" immortality from "Him who is able to grant it" if they already possessed it by nature?

First Apology 42:5 reads, "Jesus Christ, being crucified and dead, rose again, and having ascended to heaven, reigned; and by those things which were published in His name among all nations by the apostles, there is joy afforded to those who **expect** the **immortality promised** by Him." Why would Christians be said to "expect" an immortality "promised" them by Jesus if all human beings already possessed immortality by nature?

In *First Apology* 44:8, Justin says that "The sword of God is **fire**, of which they who choose to do wickedly become the **fuel**." In what theory of physics or chemistry does fire's "fuel" burn forever and never burn up?

Again, in *First Apology* 54:3, Justin says that "The ungodly among men [are] to be punished by **fire**."

Before his conversion, Justin, like many Greek philosophers, believed in Natural Immortality. In the first chapter of his *Dialogue with Trypho*, he describes Platonists as those who have "**supposed the soul to be immortal**" and therefore believe in the soul's (inherent) immortality. It is all the more instructive, therefore, to observe how vigorously he espoused Conditionalism after becoming a Christian.

The early chapters of *Dialogue with Trypho* contain Justin's testimony of how he became a Christian. After describing his previous studies in (Greek) philosophy, Justin tells of his encounter with "a certain old man" (*Dialogue with Trypho* 3:2) who shared the Gospel of Christ with him. At one point during that discussion, the "old man" asked Justin, "Is the soul ... immortal...?" (*Dialogue with Trypho* 4:7). "Assuredly," Justin replied (4:9). The entire following chapter (*Dialogue with Trypho* 5) is then devoted to the theme, "**The Soul Is Not in Its Own Nature Immortal**." In the ninth verse of this chapter, the old man asks, "They (i.e., souls) are not, then, immortal?" Driven to the only logical conclusion (after what has been said in the first eight verses), Justin replies, "No."[50]

In the following chapter (*Dialogue with Trypho* 6:7-8), the old man says, "The soul partakes of life, since God wills it to live. Thus, then, it will not even partake [of life] when God does not will it to live.... Whenever **the soul must cease to exist**, the spirit of life is removed from it, and there is no more soul."

In *Dialogue with Trypho* 12:1, Justin quotes *Isaiah* 55:3 as saying, "Hear My words, and your soul shall live" (this is an accurate quotation of the Septuagint text; the Masoretic text simply reads, "Hear, and your soul shall live"). Either way, the point is the same: "If a person does not listen, then their soul will not live. Because [they believe] it is possible for a soul to 'not live' ... it sounds as if Justin and Isaiah are not Naturalists but clearly Conditionalists."[51]

In *Dialogue with Trypho* 39:11, Justin refers to "the wicked and deceitful spirit, the serpent" (Satan), and states that he "will not cease putting to death and persecuting those who confess the name of Christ until He come again, and **destroy** them all, and render to each his deserts." Dustin Smith comments, "Here Justin is telling us that Jesus is going to return and then judge the people ... those who are judged in

---

[50] Roberts, *op. cit.*, vol. 1, 197.
[51] Smith, *op. cit.*, 6.

the negative way ... are to be destroyed ... the soul ... can in fact die, and therefore is not immortal by nature."⁵²

In *Dialogue with Trypho* 46:15, Justin says, "we [Christians]... rejoice in death, believing that God will **raise us up** by His Christ, and will **make us... immortal**...." It would be unnecessary for God to "make" an immortal soul "immortal!"

Similarly, in *Dialogue with Trypho* 69:18, Justin asserts that "if anyone be ... an observer of the doctrines delivered by [Jesus], He shall raise him up at His second advent perfectly sound, after He has **made him immortal**...." Again, it would be unnecessary for Jesus to "make" an immortal soul "immortal."

So strongly, in fact, did Justin hold this belief, that he told his Jewish friend, "If you have fallen in with some who are called Christians, but who do not admit this [truth], and venture to blaspheme the God of Abraham, and the God of Isaac, and the God of Jacob; who say there is no resurrection of the dead, and that their souls, when they die, are taken to heaven; do not imagine that they are Christians" (*Dialogue With Trypho* 80:9). This is much stronger language than most modern Conditionalists would use!

In *Dialogue with Trypho* 100:10, Justin states, "God **destroys** both the serpent [i.e., Satan] and those angels [i.e., demons] and **men** [i.e., human beings] who are like him [Satan]; but works **deliverance** from **death** to those who repent of their wickedness [i.e., Christians] and believe upon Him [i.e., Jesus]." Notice how "death" is equated with "destruction"—and how the latter (destruction) is the punishment of sinners, while the saints are "delivered" from the former (death, not eternal torment).

Similarly, in *Second Apology* 7:1, Justin says that "The wicked angels and demons and men shall **cease to exist**" in the "**destruction**

---

⁵² *Ibid.*, 7–8.

of the whole world." Dustin Smith comments, "Justin goes to great [lengths] to show us [that] there will be a time in the future when [wicked] angels, demons, and men will cease to exist. Yet according to [Naturalists] this is impossible because the soul is immortal and will live on forever either in heaven or [hell].... Justin believes that the soul ... is not immortal."[53]

In *Dialogue with Trypho* 117:6, Justin states, "He [God] shall raise all men from the dead, and appoint **some** [i.e., Christians] to be incorruptible, **immortal**, and free from sorrow in the everlasting and imperishable kingdom; but shall send **others** [i.e., non-Christians] away to **the everlasting punishment of fire**." Notice how the latter "punishment" is contrasted with the former "appointment": implying that those who are sent to the "fire" **are not** "immortal" whereas those who are appointed to the "kingdom" **are**.

In *Dialogue with Trypho* 121:11, Justin says that "On His glorious advent," Jesus will "**destroy** by all means all those who hated Him, and who unrighteously departed from Him...." ("Destroy," not "preserve alive in torment"!)

In *Address to the Greeks* 35:4, Justin urges his readers to "**learn**" from the Bible "what will **give** you **life everlasting**"—implying, of course, that if they do not learn this information, they will not have everlasting life.

There is a lengthy discussion of this topic in Justin's treatise *On the Resurrection*, which includes statements such as the following:

"The Word ... came to us ... **giving** to us **in Himself** ... eternal life..." (1:11) (implying that we did not already possess eternal life "in ourselves").

---

[53] *Ibid.*, 5.

"**Plato says** … that neither can anything be produced from what is not in being, nor anything be **destroyed** or **dissolved** into what **has not any being**," (6:3–4) (in contrast to Justin's own belief that such things **are** possible, with God).

"For as in the case of a yoke of oxen, if one or other is loosed from the yoke, neither of them can plough alone; so neither can soul or body alone effect anything," (such as continuing to live for even a moment, let alone forever!) "if they be unyoked from their communion." (8:4)

"God has **called** man to life and resurrection…" (8:18) (if "man" has to be "called" to life and resurrection, he must not be destined to them apart from such a "call").

"Those who say, that … it would not immediately follow that [the body] has the promise of the resurrection … say … the soul is incorruptible…" (8:7, 24) (in contrast to Justin's own belief that the body **does** have "the promise of the resurrection" to which to look forward, and that the soul **is** "corruptible").

"Why do we any longer endure those unbelieving and dangerous arguments, and fail to see that **we are retrograding when we listen to such an argument as this: that the soul is immortal**…? For this we used to hear from Pythagoras and Plato (who believed in Natural Immortality)…, **before** we learned the **truth** (i.e., that the soul is **mortal**)." (10:6–7)

Dustin Smith concludes, "[Justin] says many things to show that he does not believe that the soul is immortal. He also quotes passages from *the Holy Bible* that show that souls can die and that the true hope of a believer is in the future realization of the Kingdom of God. Justin's writings span over 150 pages and [he is] considered to be one of the major contributors of the Subapostolic Fathers."[54]

---

[54] Smith, *op. cit.*, 9.

Although some scholars have attempted to find traces of Neoplatonic Naturalism in Justin's writings (admittedly with a measure of success, and this, not surprisingly, considering his early education), it is the conclusion of an impressive list[55] that he was, indeed, as I have presented him as being, an outspoken Conditionalist.

Tatian of Assyria

Tatian the Apologist was born approximately AD 110 in Assyria. At first he was an eager student of heathen literature and devoted himself to the study of philosophy.[56] Then he became a pupil of Justin Martyr and was converted to Christianity. After the death of his illustrious mentor in AD 166, Tatian returned to his homeland and founded an ascetic sect called the Encratites (which means "the self-controlled ones"), which was later condemned as heretical. But Tatian himself died long before that happened, AD 180.

Of his numerous writings, the only ones that have survived are his famous *Diatessaron* (a *Harmony of the Four Gospels*, written about 175), and an *Address to the Greeks*, which is commonly referred to as the *Oratio*.

In *Oratio* 6:4, Tatian says, "Just as, not existing before I was born, I knew not who I was, and only existed in the potentiality of fleshly matter, but being born, after a former state of nothingness, I have obtained through my birth a certainty of my existence; in the same way, having been born, and **through death existing no longer**, and seen no longer, I shall exist again (i.e., after the Resurrection)."[57]

According to Tatian, "The Father who begat Him made man an image of immortality, so that, as incorruption is with God, in like

---

[55] Froom, *op. cit.*, 826–827. Note, especially, the quotation from Alger (p. 826, bottom of page).

[56] Froom, *op. cit.*, 834.

[57] Roberts, *op. cit.*, vol. 2, 67.

manner, man, sharing in a part of God, might have the immortal principle also" (*Oratio* 7:1)[58]—but, at the Fall, man was "separated from him" and became "mortal" (*Oratio* 7:7).[59] Consequently, sinful man is "fated to ... **die**" (*Oratio* 11:10).[60]

Discussing pagan mythology about astronomy, Tatian asserts that "Men, perjuring themselves for hire ... say ... that kings have ascended into heaven..." (*Oratio* 10:10). Clearly, if Tatian did not believe that "kings" go to heaven when they die, he did not assume that other "men" would. Later in the same chapter (*Oratio* 10:19), in discussing the story of "the daughter of Tyndarus," he contrasts the expression "gifted with immortality" with the expression "put to death," demonstrating again his belief that anyone who dies obviously does not possess immortality.

Oratio 13:1 makes this clear statement: "**The soul is not in itself immortal, O Greeks, but mortal.**"[61]
That Tatian did not believe in any kind of existence for disembodied souls is clear from his statement, in *Oratio* 15:2, that, "The human soul ... could [never] appear by itself without the body."

In *Oratio* 15:14, Tatian refers to the condition of men "after the **loss of immortality**." (If immortality has been "lost," men obviously no longer possess it.) Two verses later, in *Oratio* 15:16, Tatian says, "Men long for immortality." (But people don't "long for" something they already possess!)

Oratio 16:3 adds, "It is difficult to conceive that the immortal soul, which is impeded by the members of the body, should become more intelligent when it has migrated from it"[62]—thus ridiculing the common belief of those Greek philosophers, to whom Tatian was

---

[58] *Ibid.*
[59] *Ibid.*, 67–68.
[60] *Ibid.*, 69.
[61] *Ibid.*, 70.
[62] *Ibid.*, 72.

speaking, who held to the Natural Immortality doctrine. Two verses later, in *Oratio* 16:5, Tatian refers to "the divine ... power that makes souls immortal"—it would, of course, not require any "power" to "make souls immortal" if, by nature, they already were.

Referring to the final destiny of an unbeliever, Tatian says, in *Oratio* 17:2, "He ... will be delivered up in the day of consummation as fuel for the eternal fire." Fire, of course, completely destroys whatever is "delivered up" to it as "fuel." This statement is immediately followed by Tatian's warning to his reader(s), in *Oratio* 17:3, "And you ... will gain the same punishment...."

Later in the same chapter (*Oratio* 17:14–15), ridiculing the idea that "relics" of deceased saints can perform miracles, Tatian asks, "How comes it to pass that when alive I was in no wise evil, but that now **I am dead and can do nothing**, my remains, which are incapable of motion or even sense, should effect something cognizable by the senses? And **how shall he who has died** by the most miserable death **be able to assist** in avenging **any one**?"

Certainly, at least at the time he wrote the *Oratio*, Tatian, like his famous tutor, was a Conditionalist.

Theophilus of Antioch

Theophilus was born approximately AD 115 in Mesopotamia. He may have been named after the Theophilus to whom the *Gospel According to Luke* and the *Acts of the Apostles* were addressed (*Luke* 1:3; *Acts* 1:1). At any rate, he was a pupil of Polycarp of Smyrna, and served as the sixth Bishop of Antioch AD 168–180.[63] He died in Antioch in 181.

---

[63] Froom, *op. cit.*, 840–841.

Theophilus wrote to a pagan friend of his, named Autolycus, three letters which I will refer to as *1 Autolycus*, *2 Autolycus*, and *3 Autolycus*. He also wrote several other books that have since been lost.

There are many references to the subject of human immortality in the brief writings of Theophilus that we possess. For example:

1 Autolycus 7:12–13 says, "When you shall have put off the mortal, and put on incorruption, then shall you see God worthily. For God will raise your flesh immortal with your soul; and then, **having become immortal**, you shall see the Immortal, **if** now you believe on Him."[64] This is clearly Conditionalist teaching.

In *1 Autolycus* 14:7, Theophilus quotes *Romans* 2:7 (a favorite verse of many modern Conditionalists) as saying, "To those who by patient continuance in well-doing seek immortality, he will give life everlasting."[65] This is a substantially accurate quotation.

In *2 Autolycus* 15:6–7, Theophilus makes this interesting analogy: "As the sun remains ever full, never becoming less, so does God always abide perfect, being full of all power, and understanding, and wisdom, and **immortality**, and all good. But the moon wanes monthly, and in a manner **dies**, being a type of man; then it is born again, and is crescent, for a pattern of the future **resurrection**."

2 Autolycus 24:11 presents the doctrine that "Man had been made a middle nature, neither wholly mortal, nor altogether immortal, but capable of either"[66]—a teaching, again, which is favored by many Conditionalists, but is certainly not accepted by Naturalists.

This idea is developed further in *2 Autolycus* 27:1–10, which reads, "But someone will say to us, Was man made by nature mortal? Certainly not. Was he, then, immortal? Neither do we affirm this. But

---

[64] Roberts, *op. cit.*, vol. 2, 91.
[65] *Ibid.*, 93.
[66] *Ibid.*, 104.

one will say, Was he, then, Nothing? Not even this hits the mark. **He was by nature neither mortal nor immortal.** For, if He had made him immortal from the beginning, He would have made him God. Again, if He had made him mortal, God would seem to be the cause of his death. Neither, then, immortal, nor yet mortal, did He make him, but, as we have said above, capable of both; so that **if** he should incline to the things of immortality, keeping the commandment of God, he should **receive as reward** from Him immortality, and should become [as] God [is]; but **if**, on the other hand, he should turn to the things of **death**, disobeying God, he should himself be the cause of **death** to himself."[67]

Finally, in *3 Autolycus* 7:9–10, Theophilus quotes Plato as "asserting that the soul is immortal" and asks, "How can his doctrine fail to seem dreadful and monstrous—to those at least who have any judgment?"[68]

So there is no doubt at all but that Theophilus of Antioch was a Conditionalist.

Melito of Sardis

Melito the Philosopher was born early in the second century; we do not know where. He served as bishop of Sardis AD 160–177. He died around 190.[69]

Melito was a prolific writer; however, most of his treatises are known only from scanty fragments. He is best known for his *Apology to Antoninus Caesar*, written around 170, and for his *Homily on the Passover*, which was discovered in 1940.

---

[67] *Ibid.*, 105.
[68] Roberts, *op. cit.*, vol. 2, 113.
[69] Moyer, *op. cit.*, 272.

In *Apology* 7:2, Melito urges the emperor, "Believe in Him who is in reality God, and to Him lay open your mind, and to Him commit your soul, and He is able **to give you immortal life**"[70]—in verse 4, he adds, "**if** you constantly serve Him."[71]

And in *Apology* 12:5 he says, "If you follow after evil, you shall be **condemned** for your evil deeds; but … if after goodness, you shall **receive** from Him abundant good, together with **immortal life**."[72]

In *Apology* 17:14, Melito urges the emperor, "Fear Him … who can make Himself like a **fire**, and **consume** all things."

Apology 18:13–14 concludes, "At the last time, there shall be a flood of fire, and the earth shall be burnt up, together with its mountains; and **mankind shall be burnt up**, along with the idols which they have made, and the carved images which they have worshipped; and the sea shall be burnt up, together with its islands; **but the just shall be preserved** from wrath, like as were their fellows of the ark from the waters of the deluge. And then shall those who have not known God, and those who have made them idols, bemoan themselves, when they shall see those idols of theirs being **burnt up, together with themselves**, and nothing shall be found to help them."[73]

Also, in his *Homily*, Melito explains that the heritage Adam left mankind was "**not immortality** but **corruption** … **not life** but **death**…."

Clearly, what little we know of the teaching of Melito leads us to believe that he, too, was a Conditionalist.

---

[70] Roberts, *op. cit.*, vol. 8, 753.
[71] *Ibid.*
[72] *Ibid.*, 754.
[73] *Ibid.*, 755–756.

Athenagoras of Athens

Athenagoras was born in 127 in Athens. As a young philosopher, he espoused Platonism (which, of course, included the doctrine of Natural Immortality) and tried to refute the claims of Christianity. In order to do so, he studied Christian teaching in great depth. This led to his conversion. He died around 190.

The only book we now have, which we are sure was written by Athenagoras, is *A Plea for the Christians*, published in 177.[74] Another book, *A Treatise on the Resurrection of the Dead*, "is usually ascribed to him," but "some scholars have regarded it as ... written in the third, or even the fourth, century."[75]

The *Plea* makes it clear that Athenagoras was a Naturalist, even after his conversion. Part of Chapter 31 reads, "We are persuaded that when we are removed from the present life we shall live another life ... as heavenly spirit ... or, falling with the rest, a worse one and in fire; for God has not made us ... that we should perish and be annihilated." Notice that Athenagoras specifically denies that the destiny of unbelievers is to "perish," which is something that Conditionalist writers frequently affirm.

As mentioned above, we are not sure whether the *Treatise* was actually written by the same man, but clearly it reflects the same views. *Treatise* 15:2 says, "The whole nature of men in general is composed of an **immortal soul** and a body which was fitted to it in the creation."[76] And *Treatise* 15:10 adds, "Man, therefore, who consists of the two parts, must continue [to exist] forever."[77]

---

[74] Roberts, *op. cit.*, vol. 2, 127.
[75] Jerald Brauer, *The Westminster Dictionary of Church History*, Philadelphia: Westminster Press, 1971, 70–71.
[76] Roberts, *op. cit.*, vol. 2, 157.
[77] *Ibid.*

As far as we have been able to determine, Athenagoras was **the very first Christian writer** to teach the doctrine of Natural Immortality—some seventy-five years after the death of Apostle John![78] Considering his background (before his conversion), it would seem appropriate to conclude that the doctrine of the natural immortality of the soul was literally "imported" into Christianity from Platonism, rather than being any part of ancient Christian theology, as the doctrine of Conditional Immortality evidently was.

Polycrates of Ephesus

Polycrates was born approximately 125, probably in Ephesus. He was the eighth man in his family to serve as a bishop, and was bishop of Ephesus in 190, when he was excommunicated by the Bishop of Rome (Victor I) because of his stand in the Quartodeciman controversy.[79] This had nothing to do with the subject we are discussing in this book; it was a quarrel over the proper date for the celebration of Easter. Polycrates died around AD 196.

A short excerpt from his Epistle to Victor and the Roman Church Concerning the Day of Keeping the Passover is all we have of this author's writings.

The excerpt from this letter is full of references to saints of past ages as now "gone to their rest," being "laid to rest," "reposing," "resting," "lying," etc., "at" or "in" the places where they died; for example, Apostle Philip, at Hierapolis; Apostle John, at Ephesus; Thraseas of Eumenia, at Smyrna; Sagaris, at Laodicea; Melito, at Sardis; etc. Melito, in particular, is described as "awaiting the visitation from heaven, when he shall rise again from the dead."[80] The whole group thus described "shall rise again in the day of the coming of the Lord, when he comes

---

[78] Brandyberry, *op. cit.*, 8.
[79] Moyer, *op. cit.*, 331–332.
[80] Roberts, *op. cit.*, vol. 8, 774.

with glory from heaven and shall raise again all the saints."81 These are certainly phrases typically used by those who hold to a Conditionalist, not a Naturalist, view of immortality. Not a word is said of any of these "great luminaries"82 having "gone to heaven" or "continuing to live on, in the spirit world," since their death. I conclude that Polycrates of Ephesus was certainly a Conditionalist.

Irenaeus of Lyons

Irenaeus was born sometime before 130 in Smyrna. He was a pupil of Polycarp of Smyrna and served as bishop of Lyons, in Gaul (i.e., what is now known as France), from 178 until his death. Irenaeus has been described as a "second-century Fundamentalist" who believed "that Christianity can nevertheless never be a mere philosophy, that it rests rather on revelation and sacred traditions, that it acts in the Holy Spirit and is transmitted only by the Catholic (i.e., universal) Church and its apostolic word."[83] He died AD 202.[84]

In 185, Irenaeus published a five-volume treatise titled *A Refutation and Subversion of Knowledge Falsely So Called*. This work is commonly known as *Against Heresies*; I will refer to its five books as *1 Heresies*, *2 Heresies*, *3 Heresies*, *4 Heresies*, and *5 Heresies*, respectively, for the purposes of this book.

The book is full of references to the topic of human immortality. In most of these passages, Irenaeus is arguing against the Gnostic idea that the saved will live eternally as disembodied spirits; hence, he strongly emphasizes the **resurrection** and immortality of the **body**, opposing, in the process, the idea of the **innate** immortality of the **soul**. Irenaeus also introduces the expression "**confer** immortality" (to

---

[81] *Ibid.*, 773.

[82] *Ibid.*

[83] Hans Von Campenhausen, *The Fathers of the Greek Church*, New York: Pantheon Books, 1959, 27.

[84] Moyer, *op. cit.*, 204

describe God's action, which results in that which is mortal **changing** into that which is immortal), an expression which clearly contradicts the Gnostic idea of **innate** immortality. For example:

In *1 Heresies* 10:1, in a passage that may be described as "the Irenaean Creed," he states that God will "**confer** immortality on the righteous...."

In *2 Heresies* 11:1, he states that the "adoption of sons ... which is eternal life ... takes place through [Jesus] Himself, **conferring** it [i.e., eternal life] on all the righteous." (But **not**, it seems to me he implies, on the unrighteous).

In *2 Heresies* 29:2, he says, "God, when He resuscitates our **mortal bodies** which preserved righteousness, will **render them** [i.e., our **bodies**] incorruptible and **immortal**."[85]

And, "souls and spirits ... endure as long as God wills that they should have an existence and continuance" since "life does not arise from us, nor from our own nature; but it is bestowed according to the grace of God. And therefore he who shall preserve the life bestowed upon him, and give thanks to Him who imparted it, shall **receive** also length of days forever and ever. But he who shall reject it, and prove himself ungrateful to his Maker, inasmuch as he has been created, and has not recognized Him who bestowed [the gift upon him], deprives himself of [the privilege of] continuance forever and ever" (*2 Heresies* 34:3).[86] This is a pretty clear statement of the conditional nature of human immortality.

Similarly, speaking of the Gnostics, Irenaeus states, "These men ... cannot **receive** ... **immortality**." (*4 Heresies* 37:6)

---

[85] Roberts, *op. cit.*, vol. 1, 403.
[86] *Ibid.*, 411–412.

Here is another such statement: "This, therefore, was the [object of the] long-suffering of God, that man ... may know himself, how **mortal** and weak he is; while he also understands respecting God, that **He** is **immortal** and powerful to such a degree as to **confer immortality upon what is mortal** and eternity upon what is temporal; and may understand also" that "man, who had been disobedient to God," was "cast off from immortality." (*3 Heresies* 20:2)

And another: "He **grants** to those who follow and serve Him **life** and **incorruption** and **eternal** glory," *(4 Heresies* 14:1).

And another: "The Father, too, **confers** [upon man] **incorruption**" (*4 Heresies* 20:5).

And another: "Some, not knowing the power and promise of God, may oppose their own salvation, deeming it impossible for God, who raises up the dead, to have power to **confer** upon them **eternal duration**, yet the skepticism of men of this stamp shall not render the faithfulness of God of none effect." (*5 Heresies* 5:3)

And another: "**Conferring** upon them **immortality** also ... He is shown to be the only God who accomplishes these things, and as Himself the good Father, benevolently **conferring life** upon those who **have not life from themselves**." (*5 Heresies* 15:1)

And another: "[man] **receives incorruptibility** not of himself, but by the free gift of God." (*5 Heresies* 21:3)

Arguing against the heresy of the Valentinians, Irenaeus says, "They maintain ... that God ... cannot **impart immortality** to what is **mortal**..." (*2 Heresies* 14:4). Obviously, his own position is that "what is mortal" (a human being) only becomes immortal when God "imparts" immortality to it.

Again, referring to Apostle Paul, Irenaeus says, "This able wrestler, therefore, exhorts us to the **struggle** for **immortality**, that we may be crowned, and may deem the crown precious, namely, that which is **acquired** by our **struggle**, but which **does not encircle us of its own accord**." (*4 Heresies* 37:7) Clearly, this somewhat poetic language expresses Irenaeus' belief that immortality is conditional, not natural.

In a very long sentence (*4 Heresies* 11:4), Irenaeus says (among other things) that, "to scoffers, and to those not subject to God ... to those who ... are full of ... wickedness, has He assigned **everlasting perdition** by **cutting them off from life**."

Similarly, in another lengthy passage (*5 Heresies* 27:2), Irenaeus says, "Separation from God is death" (**not** "everlasting conscious torment"!) "and separation from God consists in the loss of all the benefits which He has in store." (One of those benefits, of course, is "eternal life"; so Irenaeus is clearly saying that "separation from God" equals "death" equals "the loss of eternal life.") Furthermore, he adds, "Good things are eternal and without end with God, and therefore the loss of these is also eternal and never-ending." So, according to Irenaeus, the punishment of "those ... who cast away" God's "benefits" will be a "never-ending" **loss of** eternal **life**.

Arguing with a putative questioner who asks, "Could not God have exhibited man as perfect from the beginning?" Irenaeus argues, in *4 Heresies* 38:1, that Christ "might easily have come to us in His immortal glory, but in that case we could never have endured the greatness of the glory; and therefore it was that He, who was the perfect bread of the Father, offered Himself to us as milk, [because we were] as infants. He did this when He appeared as a man, that **we**, being nourished, as it were, from the breast of His flesh, and having, by such a course of milk-nourishment, become accustomed to eat and drink the Word of God, **may be able** also **to contain in ourselves** the Bread of **immortality**, which is the Spirit of the Father"—clearly implying, of course, that **those** who are **not** so "nourished" (that is, those who do not receive Christ as Savior) are **not** able to "**contain**" in themselves the "Bread" of **immortality**.

Later in the same chapter (*4 Heresies* 38:3), Irenaeus refers to "the gratuitous **bestowal** of **eternal existence** upon [believers] by God" and states that "being in subjection to God is continuance in immortality" and that "the beholding of God is productive of immortality" (implying that rebellion against God, and failure to "behold" God, lead to the opposite of immortality, continuance in nonexistence).

In *5 Heresies* 29:1, Irenaeus describes the process of being "saved" as a "**ripening** for immortality"—obviously, fruits do not "ripen" into a condition in which they already exist. Put another way, it could be said that a Naturalist would be unlikely to use such an expression.

Irenaeus also uses the typically Conditionalist words "destroy" and "destruction" (specifically, "by fire") to describe the destiny of the unsaved. For example:

In *2 Heresies* 32:2, speaking of those Gnostics who, believing "that it is incumbent on them to have experience of every kind of work; but, turning aside to voluptuousness, and lust, and abominable actions ... stand ... condemned," he says, "since they are destitute of all those [virtues] which have been mentioned [i.e., earlier in the passage], they will [of necessity] pass into the **destruction** of **fire**."

Similarly, "Those who do these things, since they do indeed walk after the flesh, have not the power of living unto God ... Man goes to **destruction**, if he has continued to live after the flesh." (*5 Heresies* 11:1)

Interestingly, however, in quoting *2 Thessalonians* 1:9, in *4 Heresies* 33:11, Irenaeus substitutes the word "death" for the word usually translated as "destruction"—rendering *2 Thessalonians* 1:9 as, "Who shall be punished with **everlasting death** from the face of the Lord, and from the glory of His power."

In another interesting quotation (quoting 2 *Corinthians* 5:4, in *4 Heresies* 36:6), Irenaeus substitutes the word "immortality" for the word usually translated as "life"—rendering 2 *Corinthians* 5:4 as, "Not for that we would be unclothed, but clothed upon, that mortality might be swallowed up by **immortality**."

In still another (quoting *John* 3:36, in *4 Heresies* 37:5), Irenaeus— significantly, it would seem—inserts the word "eternal" in a place where it is not found in the Biblical text, rendering *John* 3:36 as, "He that believeth in Him has eternal life; while he who believeth not the Son hath not **eternal** life, but the wrath of God shall remain upon him." This could be said to be a very "Conditionalist" way of "interpreting" the actual text of *John* 3:36.

Other "Conditionalist" statements by Irenaeus are as follows:

"Men ... are ... **mortal**...." (*2 Heresies* 7:1)

"The soul, ... while ... sharing life with the body ... does not ... cease to live." (*2 Heresies* 33:4)—implying, it seems, that when the body ceases to live, the soul also ceases to live.

"The unbelieving ... shall not inherit ... life...." (*3 Heresies* 7:2)

"Those who ... are in a state of death ... are deprived of His gift, which is eternal life...; they remain ... **mortal**." (*3 Heresies* 19:1)

"Man should never adopt an opposite opinion with regard to God, supposing that the incorruptibility which belongs to him is his own naturally, and by thus not holding the truth, should boast with empty superciliousness, as if he were naturally like to God." (*3 Heresies* 20:1)

"Those who ... are outside the kingdom of God ... are disinherited from [the gift of] incorruption...." (*4 Heresies* 8:1)

"But the Word of God did not accept of the friendship of Abraham, as though He stood in need of it, for He was perfect from the beginning ("Before Abraham was," He says, "I am"), but that He in His goodness might **bestow eternal life** upon Abraham himself, inasmuch as the friendship of God **imparts immortality** to those who embrace it." (*4 Heresies* 13:4)

"God has always preserved freedom, and the power of self-government in man, while at the same time He issued His own exhortations, in order that **those who do not obey Him** should be righteously judged (**condemned**) because they have not obeyed Him; and that **those who have** obeyed and **believed on Him** should be honored with **immortality**." (*4 Heresies* 15:2)

"Thus man might **attain** to **immortality**...." (*4 Heresies* 20:2)

"Those, therefore, who see God, do **receive life**. And for this reason, He, [although] beyond comprehension, and boundless and invisible, rendered Himself visible, and comprehensible, and within the capacity of those who believe, that He might **vivify** those who **receive** and behold Him through faith.... He **bestows life** upon those who see Him. It is **not possible to live** apart from **life**, and the means of **life** is found in fellowship with God"; (*4 Heresies* 20:5).

"Men therefore shall see God, that they may **live**, being **made immortal** by that sight," (*4 Heresies* 20:6).

"Man, falling away from God altogether, [will] **cease to exist**." (*4 Heresies* 20:7).

"They who believe in Him shall be **incorruptible**...." (*4 Heresies* 24:2)

"They all received a penny each man, having [stamped upon it] the royal image and superscription, the knowledge of the Son of God, which is **immortality**." (*4 Heresies* 36:7)

"It is good to obey God, and **to believe in Him**, and to keep His commandment, and this **is** the **life** of man; as **not to obey God** is evil, and this **is** his **death** ... it is an evil thing which **deprives him of life**, that is, disobedience to God ... what **preserves his life**, namely, obedience to God, is good.... How, again, can he be **immortal**, who in his **mortal** nature did not obey his Maker?... If you, being obstinately hardened, do reject the operation of His skill, and show yourself ungrateful towards Him, because you were created a [mere] man, by becoming thus ungrateful to God, you have at once **lost** both His workmanship and **life**." (*4 Heresies* 39:1–2)

"But when they should be converted and come to repentance, and cease from evil, they should have power to become the sons of God, and to **receive** the inheritance of **immortality** which is **given** by Him." (*4 Heresies* 41:3)

"The Father ... **gives** to this mortal **immortality**, and to this corruptible incorruption ... in order that we may never become puffed up, **as if we had life from ourselves**, and exalted against God, our minds becoming ungrateful; but learning by experience that we possess **eternal duration** from the excelling power of this Being, **not** from **our own nature**." (*5 Heresies* 2:3)

"Man ... is ... **mortal** by nature." (*5 Heresies* 3:1)

"**Incorruption** ... is a blissful and **never-ending life**" which is "**granted** by God." (*5 Heresies* 3:3)

"He cuts away the lusts of the flesh, those which bring **death** upon a man." (*5 Heresies* 10:2)

The "works of the flesh ... bring **death** [upon their doers]." (*5 Heresies* 11:2)

"**Death** brings **mortality**." (*5 Heresies* 12:1)

"**God** is He who **gives** ... **immortality**." (*5 Heresies* 13:3)

"Carnal deeds..., perverting man to sin, **deprive him of life**." (*5 Heresies* 14:4)

There is no question but that Irenaeus of Lyons was a "champion"[87] of Conditionalism. We see, then, that the age of the Subapostolic Fathers comes to its conclusion at a point in time prior to which **only one** Christian writer (Athenagoras) has espoused the doctrine of Natural Immortality, **all the others** (of whom we have studied a total of seventeen) having held, more or less demonstrably, to Conditionalism.

The Ante-Nicene Fathers

As mentioned previously, the Ante-Nicene Fathers who wrote on the subject of Human Immortality were:

Clement of Alexandria (AD 153–213?)
Tertullian of Carthage (AD 145–220)
Hippolytus of Portus Romanus (AD 170–236)
The writer(s) of the *Pseudo-Clementines* (approximately AD 220)
Minucius Felix of Africa (AD 185–250)
Origen of Alexandria (AD 185–254)
Commodianus of Africa (AD 200–275)
Cyprian of Carthage (AD 200–258)
Novatian of Rome (AD 210–280)
Gregory Thaumaturgus of Neocaesarea (AD 213–270)
Arnobius of Sicca (AD 250–327)

Their writings cover approximately the third century (AD).

---

[87] Froom, *op. cit.*, 873.

Clement of Alexandria

Titus Flavius Clemens was born in 153 in Athens, of pagan parents.[88] "Originally a pagan philosopher," he traveled extensively in Greece, Italy, Egypt, Palestine, and other countries, then studied Christian Gnosticism from 180–189 at the school founded by Pantaenus of Alexandria.[89] When Pantaenus retired (to go into missionary work), Clement became headmaster of the school, and he continued in that position from AD 189–202. He fled Alexandria in 202 as a result of the persecution of Christians which occurred during the reign of Septimius Severus. Later, he again traveled rather extensively. We do not know the circumstances of his death, which occurred sometime between 211 and 215.[90]

While he was headmaster in Alexandria, Clement wrote three major treatises: *Protrepticus* (or *An Exhortation to the Heathen*)— approximately AD 190; *Paedogogus* (or *The Instructor*)— approximately AD 192; and *Stromata* (or *Miscellaneous Teachings*)— approximately AD 194.

Clement also wrote several other books that now exist only in fragments, including one titled *Hypotyposes* (or *Illustrations*). It is unclear whether this book was written earlier than *Protrepticus*, *Paedogogus*, and *Stromata* (as Anne Mbeke suggests) or later (as LeRoy Froom believes). The answer to this question could have a considerable impact on the interpretation of Clement's possible change in position, which will be discussed, briefly, below.

Clement is also credited with authoring "the oldest Christian hymn of which the authorship is known,"[91] the English translation

---

[88] Anne Mbeke, *Clement of Alexandria and Conditional Immortality*, Charlotte: Venture Books, 2006, 2.

[89] Moyer, *op. cit.*, 94.

[90] Von Campenhausen, *op. cit.*, 38.

[91] Kenneth W. Osbeck, *Amazing Grace: 366 Inspiring Hymn Stories for Daily Devotions*, Grand Rapids: Kregel Publications, 1990, 81.

of which is titled, "Shepherd of Eager Youth." It was "used as a hymn of Christian instruction for new young converts from heathenism."

Despite the large quantity of material that Clement has left us, there are relatively few references in his writings to the subject of human immortality, and those that there are, are not very clear. For example, in *Paedogogus* 1:3, he says, "Let us regard the Word as law, and His commands and counsels as the short and straight paths to immortality." In *Paedogogus* 1:6, he says, "Being baptized, we are illuminated; illuminated, we become sons; being made sons, we are made perfect; being made perfect, we are **made immortal,**" and "the spiritual communion of faith ... **commits** man to **eternity** ... **immortalizing** him." These certainly sound like the words of a Conditionalist. But in *Stromata*, Book IV, Chapter 3, he says, "Death ... is the dissolution of the chains which bind the soul to the body." This certainly sounds like the teaching of a Naturalist. And in the fragment of a lost work titled *On the Soul*, Clement is quoted as saying, "All souls are immortal, even of the godless, to whom it were better not to be incorruptible." Here, too, Clement does appear to be a Naturalist; but, in other fragments, he appears to be a Conditionalist. LeRoy Edwin Froom says (but without documenting it) that Clement "changed" from Conditionalist to Naturalist;[92] he also classifies him with those Naturalists who held to the teaching of "Universal Restoration."[93] Anne Mbeke, on the other hand, speculates "that Clement changed his mind, but from a Naturalist to a Conditionalist, and not vice versa." Perhaps it would be better, then, for the purposes of this book, not to classify Clement of Alexandria as either a Naturalist or a Conditionalist, but to leave him unclassified until further research can be completed.

---

[92] Froom, *op. cit.*, 758.
[93] *Ibid.*

Tertullian of Carthage

Quintus Septimius Florens Tertullianus was born approximately AD 145 in Carthage.[94] He became a Christian around 185 and an elder in the church at Carthage about five years later, and was one of the Church's most prolific writers from then until his conversion to Montanism, for which he was excommunicated. Tertullian died around AD 220.[95]

A bare listing of just the titles of his best-known works, together with the dates when they were written, would have to include at least the following:

On Repentance, AD 195
On Baptism, AD 195
On Prayer, AD 195
Apology, AD 197
To the Martyr, AD 197
On the Shows, AD 197
An Answer to the Jews, AD 198
Prescription against Heretics, AD 200
On Patience, AD 202
On the Apparel of Women, AD 202
On Penitence, AD 203
On the Soul, AD 203
The Chaplet, AD 204
Exhortation to Chastity, AD 204
Antidote for the Scorpion's Sting, AD 205
Against Marcion, AD 207
To My Wife, AD 207
Against Hermogenes, AD 207
Against the Valentinians, AD 207
On the Flesh of Christ, AD 207

---

[94] Roberts, *op. cit.*, vol. 3, 3.
[95] *Ibid.*, 4.

On the Veiling of Virgins, AD 207
Against Praxeas, AD 208
On the Pallium, AD 208
On Monogamy, AD 208
On Modesty, AD 208
On Fasting, AD 208
On the Resurrection of the Flesh, AD 208

In many of these books, Tertullian discusses the question of human immortality. He says, for example, "All who are not true worshipers of God ... shall be consigned to the punishment of everlasting fire ... which ... does not consume what it scorches, but while it burns it repairs." (*Apology* 48:31–33) This graphic description of the torment of the unsaved clearly is based on the assumption of their unending existence.

Again, he says clearly, "The soul, then, we define to be ... immortal." (*On the Soul* 22:5)

Furthermore, Tertullian adds, "We ... maintain ... that souls are even now susceptible of torment and of blessing in Hades, though they are disembodied." (*On the Resurrection* 17:2–3)

A few sentences later, he adds, "The soul ... has no ... mortality." (*On the Resurrection* 18:17)

And, in *On the Resurrection* 35:2, Tertullian used the phrase "**the natural immortality of the soul**," probably for the first time in any Christian writing.

Obviously, Quintus Septimius Florens Tertullianus must be classified as a Naturalist; indeed, there is a sense in which he should be regarded as one of the "Founding Fathers" of the doctrine of Natural Immortality.

Hippolytus of Portus Romanus

Hippolytus was born approximately AD 170; we do not know where.[96] He was a pupil of Irenaeus of Lyons. For the first third of the third century, he served as Bishop of Portus, which was a suburb of Rome. He died by drowning in 236.[97]

Hippolytus is credited with many writings, including the following:

The Little Labyrinth;
On Christ and Antichrist;
Against the Jews;
Against Noetus;
Against Beron and Helix;
On the Holy Theophany;
Against Plato; and
The Refutation of All Heresies.

He may also have been the author of the famous and mysterious *Letter to Diognetus*, which was preserved in a single manuscript dating from the thirteenth or fourteenth century and published in AD 1592. The manuscript itself no longer exists, having been destroyed in a fire AD 1870. The intended recipient of this fine example of an early Christian "apology" (a defense of the Christian religion against attacks by paganism) may have been the Diognetus who was the tutor of the Roman emperor Marcus Aurelius. It contains a description of the lifestyle of the early Christians (*Diognetus* 5) and the explicit statement, "The soul, which is immortal, lives in a mortal dwelling" (*Diognetus* 6:8).

---

[96] William McDonald, *The New Catholic Encyclopedia*, New York: McGraw-Hill, 1967, vol. 6, 1139.
[97] Roberts, *op. cit.*, vol. 5, 6.

Against Plato 1:6 says that "The unrighteous, and those who believed not God, who have honored as God the vain works of the hands of men, idols fashioned (by themselves), shall be sentenced to this **endless punishment** [in the lake of fire]." Later in the same book, Hippolytus says that "The lovers of iniquity shall be given **eternal punishment**. And the fire which is unquenchable and without end awaits the latter, and a certain fiery worm which does not die, and which does not waste the body, but continues bursting forth from the body with unending pain. No sleep will give them rest; no night will soothe them; **no death** will deliver them from punishment." (*Against Plato* 3:6–8)

Furthermore, in the *Refutation*, Hippolytus specifically criticizes:

1) the Naassenes, for believing in the existence of a "mortal soul" (Book V, Chapter;
2) Tatian of Assyria (whom we have seen was a Conditionalist), as a "heretic" (Book VIII, Chapter 9);
3) the Quartodecimans (among whom was Polycrates of Ephesus, an outspoken Conditionalist), as "heretics" (Book VIII, Chapter 11); and
4) the Sadducees, for supposing "that the soul does not continue after death," "that there will be a dissolution both of soul and body," and "that man passes into nonexistence."

Obviously, Hippolytus of Portus Romanus was both a Naturalist and an outspoken opponent of Conditionalism and of many of the early Church Fathers who held to it.

The Writer(s) of the *Pseudo-Clementines*

The so-called *Pseudo-Clementines* are a group of books written around 220 by an unknown, probably Jewish Christian, author or group of authors.[98] They are designed to look as if they were written by Clement of Rome, but, clearly, they were not. Three of the books are known, respectively, as the *Recognitions*, the *Homilies*, and the *Epitome*.[99]

According to the author(s) of the *Pseudo-Clementines*, "**The soul is immortal**" (*1 Recognitions* 5:6). *3 Recognitions* 39–49 is an eleven-chapter-long "proof" of the immortality of the soul. *5 Recognitions* 28:2 specifies that "Even the souls of the impious are immortal, though perhaps they themselves would wish them to end with their bodies."[100] *8 Recognitions* 28:3–4 explains that "although man consists of different substances, one mortal and the other immortal, yet, by the skillful contrivance of the Creator, their diversity does not prevent their union, and that although the substances be diverse and alien the one from the other. For the one is taken from the earth and formed by the Creator, but the other is given from immortal substances; and yet the honor of its immortality is not violated by this union."[101]

The same teaching is equally prominent in the *Homilies*. *1 Homily* 5:3 says that "**The soul is immortal**"; *2 Homily* 13:1 insists that "There is every necessity, that he who says that God is by His nature righteous, should believe also that **the souls of men are immortal**: for where would be His justice, when some, having lived piously, have been evil-treated, and sometimes violently cut off, while others who have been wholly impious, and have indulged in luxurious living, have died the common death of men?"[102] The rest of the chapter goes on to say, "Since therefore, without all contradiction, God who is good is also just, He shall not otherwise be known to be just, unless the soul after its separation from the body be immortal, so that the wicked man, being in hell, as having here received his good things, may there be punished for his sins; and the good man, who has been punished here

---

[98] Froom, *op. cit.*, 758.
[99] Roberts, *op. cit.*, vol. 8, 69.
[100] *Ibid.*, 150.
[101] Roberts, *op. cit.*, vol. 8, 173.
[102] *Ibid.*, 231.

for his sins, may then, as in the bosom of the righteous, be constituted an heir of good things. Since therefore God is righteous, it is fully evident to us that there is a judgment, and that **souls are immortal**."[103] *2 Homily* 29–31 is a three-chapter-long "proof" of the immortality of the soul, and *11 Homily* 11:2 insists that "**the soul** even of the wicked **is immortal**, for whom it were better not to have it incorruptible." The next verse adding, "For, being punished with **endless torture** under unquenchable fire, and **never dying**, it can receive **no end** of its misery."[104]

It is clear that whoever wrote these books (and tried to pass them off as if they had actually been written by Clement, who, as we have seen, was a Conditionalist!) was, or were, believer(s), in the doctrine of Natural Immortality.

Minucius Felix of Africa

Minucius Felix Marcus was probably born around AD 185 in Africa. As a young man, he was converted from paganism to Christianity.[105] He died approximately 250 in Rome.[106]

Sometime during the first half of the third century, Minucius Felix wrote an *Apology* in the form of a discussion between a pagan named Caecilius (nowadays we would call him "Cecil") and a Christian named Octavius. The work is generally known as the *Octavius*.

Octavius 35:1 describes the punishment of the wicked as "**eternal torments**"; *Octavius* 35:3 specifies, "Nor is there either measure or termination to these torments." The next verse adds, "The intelligent fire burns the limbs and restores them, feeds on them and nourishes them." And the following verse concludes, "As **the fires** of the

---

[103] *Ibid.*
[104] *Ibid.*, 286.
[105] Roberts, *op. cit.*, vol. 4, 170.
[106] McDonald, *op. cit.*, vol. 9, 883.

thunderbolts strike upon the bodies, and **do not consume them**; as the fires of Mount Aetna and of Mount Vesuvius, and of burning lands (i.e., volcanoes) everywhere, glow, but are not wasted; so that penal fire (i.e., Hell) is not fed by the waste of those who burn, but is nourished by the unexhausted eating away of their bodies."[107] Although none of the actual terms "immortal," "immortality," "soul," etc., is actually used in these verses, it is clear that this doctrine of Hell is based on the assumption of the innate immortality of the human soul. No one will express any surprise at my conclusion that Minucius Felix was a Naturalist.

Origen of Alexandria

Origen Adamantinus (this nickname means "hard as a rock") was born approximately AD 185 in Alexandria, the oldest of the seven sons of Leonides, who was martyred under the persecution that arose under Emperor Septimius Severus.[108] He was a pupil of Clement of Alexandria (and also of Ammonius Saccas, a Neoplatonist), and taught Christianity (among other subjects)—first, at Alexandria, AD 203–231 (when he was excommunicated by the Bishop of Alexandria), and then at Caesarea, AD 231–249 (when he was imprisoned during the persecution that arose under Emperor Decian). He died in AD 254 at Tyre.[109]

Origen's first (and greatest) work was a book known in Greek as *Peri Archon*, in Latin as *De Principiis*, and in English as *On the Principles*, which he published around 215. Other major works include the following:

On the Resurrection;
On Prayer;

---

[107] Roberts, *op. cit.*, vol. 4, 195.
[108] Roberts, *op. cit.*, vol. 4, 224.
[109] *Ibid.*, 229.

Commentary on John (AD 230–238);
Exhortation to Martyrdom (AD 232);
Letter to Gregory Thaumaturgus (AD 235);
Letter to Julius Africanus (AD 240);
Dialogue with Heraclides (AD 246);
Against Celsus (AD 247);
Commentary on Matthew (AD 247);
Homily on Ezekiel;
Homily on Leviticus; and
Apology (AD 248)
… to name just a few!

However, one need read no more than *De Principiis* to ascertain Origen's position on the subject of human immortality.

In the Introduction, he states that "The soul, having a substance and life of its own, shall, after its departure from the world, be rewarded according to its desserts, being destined to obtain either an inheritance of eternal life and blessedness, if its actions shall have procured this for it, or to be delivered up to **eternal fire and punishments**, if the guilt of its crimes shall have brought it down to this."[110]

Later, in *Book II*, 2:1, he says that "spiritual and rational minds, will be … eternal…."

And, in the same *Book*, 10:1, he comments that it would be "vain and superfluous for anyone to arise from the dead in order to die a second time."[111] This is exactly what most Conditionalists teach will happen.

Furthermore, "the body which rises again of those who are to be destined to **everlasting fire** or to severe punishments, is by the very

---

[110] *Ibid.*, 240.
[111] *Ibid.*, 294.

change of the resurrection so incorruptible, that **it cannot be** corrupted and **dissolved** even by severe punishments" (*Book II*, 10:3).[112]

In *Book IV*, 1:36, Origen asserts that "**the human soul will also be immortal.**"[113]

And, in *Against Celsus, Book III*, 22:5, he claims that "**the doctrine of the soul's immortality** ... is to us a doctrine of preeminent importance."[114]

In the same work, *Book VI*, 71:5, he concludes that "We, however, know of no incorporeal substance that is destructible by fire, **nor [do we believe] that the soul of man**, or the substance of 'angels,' or of 'thrones,' or 'dominions,' or 'principalities,' or 'powers,' **can be dissolved by fire**."[115]

Clearly, Origen of Alexandria was both a Naturalist and a fine and well-known spokesman of the doctrine of Natural Immortality.

Indeed, the Early Church historian, Eusebius of Caesarea (AD 263–339), in his *History of the Church*, Book VI, Chapter 37, tells how Origen disputed with some Thnetopsychites—("the sect that proclaimed the mortality of the soul")—at a "synod of no small dimensions" in Arabia in 246. No writings by any member of this group have been preserved, but obviously they were Conditionalists. Eusebius describes them as "saying that the human soul dies." One of them, Demetrius, was a bishop, and is quoted in Origen's *Dialogue with Heraclides*, chapter 167, as criticizing Origen for teaching "that **the soul is immortal**." Thus, both in Eusebius' history, and in Origen's own writings, there is preserved a record of the fact that in the middle of the third century, both Natural Immortality and Conditional Immortality were being taught in Christian churches, and

---

[112] Roberts, *op. cit.*, 294–295.
[113] *Ibid.*, 381.
[114] *Ibid.*, 472.
[115] *Ibid.*, 606.

there was an active, ongoing debate between the proponents of the two positions.

Commodianus of Africa

Commodianus Mendicus Christi (this nickname means "the servant of Christ") was born approximately AD 200 in North Africa. Little is known about his life and work except that he was apparently serving as a bishop somewhere in North Africa around 240, when he wrote a poem called *Instructions in Favor of Christian Discipline*.[116] He died approximately AD 275;[117] we do not know where, or under what circumstances.

The *Instructions* contain two references to the subject of human immortality:

1) "I … thought … that when once life had departed, the soul also was dead and perished. These things, however, are not so…." (*Instructions* 26:13–14)
2) "O fool, you do not absolutely die; nor, when dead, do you escape the lofty One … You are stripped, O foolish one, who thinks that by death you are not…." (*Instructions* 278:1,7)

These statements clearly demonstrate that Commodianus was a Naturalist.

Cyprian of Carthage

Thascius Caecilius Cyprian was born approximately AD 200 near Carthage.[118] He was converted to Christianity in 246 and served as

---

[116] Roberts, *op. cit.*, vol. 4, 201.
[117] Moyer, *op. cit.*, 99.
[118] Moyer, *op. cit.*, 108.

bishop of Carthage AD 248–258.[119] He was executed in AD 258 for refusing to deny Christ.[120]

Some of the more famous of Cyprian's hundreds of writings include the following, together with their dates of publication, if known:

Letter to Donatus (AD 246);
The Vanity of Idols (AD 247);
Against the Jews (AD 248);
Concerning the Lapsed (AD 251);
The Unity of the Church (AD 251);
Commentary on the Lord's Prayer (AD 252);
Address to Demetrianus (AD 252);
Concerning Mortality (AD 252);
Works and Alms (AD 254);
Jealousy and Envy (AD 256); and
The Glory of Martyrdom.

Despite the tremendous quantity of material Cyprian has left us (the more remarkable as he produced it in a period of only ten years, and while serving as bishop of a major Christian community), there are few references to the subject of human immortality in his writings. These few occur primarily in the treatises *Concerning Mortality* and *The Glory of Martyrdom.*

In *Mortality* 14:3 he says, "He … who … is delivered over to the fires of Gehenna … eternal flame shall **torment** with **never-ending** punishments…." This is certainly the language of Naturalism.

In the *Martyrdom*, however, Cyprian's position is not nearly as clear. *Martyrdom* 8:5 says, "Doubtless let that lust of life keep hold, but let it be of those whom for unatoned sin the raging fire will **torture** with **eternal vengeance** for their crimes."[121]

---

[119] Roberts, *op. cit.*, vol. 5, 264.
[120] Moyer, *op. cit.*, 108.
[121] Roberts, *op. cit.*, vol. 5, 581.

And *Martyrdom* 10:4 refers to the eventuality of "being punished with a **perpetual burning**."[122]

But in the very next chapter, Cyprian says that "The fire will **consume** those who are enemies of the truth. The paradise of God blooms for the witnesses; Gehenna will enfold the deniers, and eternal fire will **burn them up**" (*Martyrdom* 11:4–5).[123]

This last reference sounds more like the words of a Conditionalist! Dr. Froom, however, classifies Cyprian as a Naturalist;[124] and, on the strength of the unequivocal statement in *Mortality* 14:3, I will, at least tentatively, do the same.

Novatian of Rome

Novatian was born in 210; his birthplace is unknown, possibly Phrygia.[125] He was serving as an elder in the church at Rome when a split occurred, in 251, over the question of recommunicating those who had left the church during a time of persecution (Cyprian of Carthage referred to this situation in his *Treatise Concerning the Lapsed*). Novatian took a "hard line," left the Catholic Church, and founded a sect called the Catharoi (a word which means the same thing as the English word "Puritans"). He served as its bishop until his martyrdom AD 280. The Catharoi (not to be confused with the Cathari of a later era!) continued as a separate denomination until sometime in the sixth century.[126]

Prior to AD 250, Novatian had written at least two "letters,"[127] which have not been preserved. He wrote a *Treatise on the Jewish*

---

[122] Roberts, *op. cit.*, vol. 5, 581.
[123] *Ibid.*
[124] Froom, *op. cit.*, 758.
[125] Froom, *op. cit.*, 902–903.
[126] Moyer, *op. cit.*, 303.
[127] Referenced in his *Treatise on the Jewish Meats* 1:7.

Meats in 250. He also wrote a *Treatise Concerning the Trinity* in 257. The former book contains one reference to the subject of human immortality; the latter book contains several.

In *Jewish Meats* 5:18, Novatian quotes Christ as saying, "But labor not for the meat which perisheth, but for the meat which endureth to **life eternal**, which the Son of man will give you; for him hath the Father sealed" (John 6:27). This is a substantially accurate quotation of a verse popular among modern Conditionalists who follow the interpretation that makes the word "which" refer to the phrase "life eternal" rather than to the word "meat."

In *Trinity* 1, Novatian describes the "punishment" for Adam's disobedience to God's command not to eat "the fruit of the tree" of the knowledge of good and evil as being "mortality."

Once in *Trinity* 2, once in *Trinity* 3, three times in *Trinity* 4, once in *Trinity* 6, and once in *Trinity* 31, Novatian states that God is "immortal";[128] but in *Trinity* 15:28 he says that "every man is mortal" and adds that "immortality cannot be from that which is mortal."[129]

In *Trinity* 14:12, he describes the punishment for denying Christ as "**destruction** of the soul," and in *Trinity* 14:15–16 goes on to say, "If Christ is only man, how is it that 'even as the Father hath life in Himself, so hath He given to the Son to have life in Himself,' when **man cannot have life** in him after the example of God the Father, **because he is** not glorious in eternity, but **made with the materials of mortality**? If Christ is only man, how does He say, 'I am the bread of eternal life which came down from heaven,' when **man** can neither be the bread of life, **he himself being mortal**, nor could he have come down from heaven, since no perishable material is established in heaven?"[130] Here Novatian bases an argument for Christ's divinity on

---

[128] Roberts, *op. cit.*, vol. 5, 612–615.
[129] *Ibid,* 624.
[130] Roberts, *op. cit.*, vol. 5, 623.

the very distinction between Deity and humanity, that Deity is by nature immortal, and humanity is not immortal.

Similarly, in *Trinity* 15:38, he says that "Every man is bound by the laws of **mortality**, and therefore is unable to keep himself [alive] forever."[131]

Furthermore, in *Trinity* 16:2–3, he refers to the punishment of unbelief as being "to **die** for evermore" and to "**die** eternally," while, in *Trinity* 16:4, he says, by way of contrast, that the **believer** (and he only) is "destined for the attainment of everlasting **life**."[132]

And in *Trinity* 18:37, he refers to "the **destruction** of the people of Sodom" (notice, he does not say, "the destruction of the **city**," but, "the destruction of the **people**").

The above quotations make it clear that, as Dr. Froom says, "Novatian was a Conditionalist."[133]

What, then, are we to make of *Trinity* 25:9–17, which contains the following statements: "For **what if** the divinity in Christ does not die, but the substance of the flesh only is destroyed, **when** in other men also, who are not flesh only, but flesh and soul, the flesh indeed alone suffers the inroads of wasting and death, **while** the soul **is seen** to be uncorrupted, and beyond the laws of destruction and death?" (v. 9); "**if** the immortal soul cannot be killed…" (v. 11); "**if** in any man whatever, the soul has this excellence of immortality **that** it cannot be slain…" (v. 12); "**if** the cruelty of man fails to destroy the soul…" (v. 13); "the soul itself … is not killed by men" (v. 14); and "**if** … death … does not destroy the soul, **although** it dissolves the bodies themselves: for it could exercise its power on the bodies, it did not avail to exercise it on the souls; for the one in them was mortal, and therefore died; the other in them was

---

[131] *Ibid.*, 625.
[132] *Ibid.*
[133] Froom, *op. cit.*, 909.

immortal, and therefore **is understood** not to have been extinguished" (v. 17)? The abundance of words such as "what if," "when," "while," "is seen," "if," "if ... that," "if," "if ... although" and "is understood" leads me to suggest that Novatian is here using a form of argument in which he concedes to his readers **"for the sake of argument"** certain assumptions he knows they will admit, which will enable him to convince them of his point, though he does not hold those assumptions as part of his own belief system (as demonstrated elsewhere).

In *Trinity* 29:25–27, Novatian clearly ties human immortality to the resurrection of human **bodies** (as opposed to survival of human **souls**): "[The Holy Spirit is] an inhabitant given for our **bodies** and an effector of **their** holiness. Who, working for us in eternity, can also produce our **bodies** at the **resurrection** of **immortality**.... For our **bodies** are both trained in Him and by Him to advance to **immortality**, by learning to govern themselves with moderation according to His decrees."

Novatian was called a "heretic" by Cyprian of Carthage (and others, including the anonymous author of the *Treatise against the Heretic Novatian*, which was written in 255 in Africa), but not because of his position on immortality; rather, because of his strict approach to recommunication, which resulted in his break with the more "soft line" Catholicism. Indeed, the author of the *Treatise against the Heretic Novatian* was probably himself a Conditionalist; he frequently uses the word "destruction" to refer to the destiny of the unsaved, and quotes several Scriptures often used by modern Conditionalists, such as Ezekiel 18:4,20–21; Matthew 10:28; Luke 18:1–5; Jude 15 (which he alters to read, "to execute judgment upon all, and to **destroy** all the wicked," etc.); and Revelation 6:17 (which he alters to read, "because the day of **destruction** cometh," etc.).

Gregory Thaumaturgus of Neocaesarea

Gregory Thaumaturgus (this nickname means the "Miracle-Worker") was born in 213 in Neocaesarea, Pontus.[134] He was raised in a pagan home, studying Neoplatonic philosophy and Roman law, but was converted to Christianity by the teaching of Origen of Alexandria in 233. Five years later, he returned to his home town, found seventeen Christians there, and organized them into a church. He then served as bishop of Neocaesarea from AD 240[135] until his death in 270, at Neocaesarea,[136] by which time it was said (perhaps in exaggeration) that there were only seventeen pagans left in the city!

Here are the titles of some of Gregory's writings:

Declaration of Faith;
Metaphrase of the Book of Ecclesiastes;
Oration and Panegyric Addressed to Origen (AD 238);
Canonical Epistle (AD 258–262);
Sectional Confession of Faith;
On the Trinity;
Twelve Topics on the Faith;
On the Subject of the Soul;
Four Homilies;
On All the Saints; and
On the Gospel According to Matthew.

A quick reading of *On the Subject of the Soul* will easily establish Gregory's position on the question of human immortality. The entire sixth chapter is devoted to the question of "whether our soul is immortal." Verse 3 concludes that "The soul, being simple, and not being made up of diverse parts, but being uncompound and indissoluble, must be, in virtue of that, incorruptible and immortal."[137]

---

[134] McDonald, *op. cit.*, vol. 6, 797.
[135] Roberts, *op. cit.*, vol. 6, 3.
[136] See also Moyer, *op. cit.*, 171.
[137] Roberts, *op. cit.*, vol. 6, 56.

Verse 5 adds that "The soul, being self-acting, has no cessation of its being."[138] Verses 6–7 reason that "It follows that what is self-acting is ever-acting; and what is ever-acting is unceasing; and what is unceasing is without end; and what is without end is incorruptible; and what is incorruptible is immortal. Consequently, [since] the soul is self-acting, as has been shown above, it follows that it is incorruptible and immortal."[139] Verse 10 reiterates, "[Since], therefore, the soul is not corrupted by the evil proper to itself, and the evil of the soul is cowardice, intemperance, envy, and the like, and all these things do not despoil it of its powers of life and action, it follows that it is immortal."

So there is no question but that Gregory Thaumaturgus, like his teacher, Origen of Alexandria, was a Naturalist.

Arnobius of Sicca

Arnobius the Elder was born approximately AD 250. He lived in Sicca, Numidia, North Africa. As a pagan, he was noted for his intense hatred of Christianity. He was converted around AD 303, but he was at first distrusted (like Saul, in *Acts* 9:26), and was refused baptism. This led to his publication of a series of seven books collectively titled *Disputations Against the Pagans* sometime between AD 303 and AD 310.[140] I will refer to these books as *1 Disputations*, *2 Disputations*, *3 Disputations*, *4 Disputations*, *5 Disputations*, *6 Disputations*, and *7 Disputations*, respectively, for the purposes of this book. Arnobius died around AD 327.[141]

In *1 Disputations* 18:5, Arnobius says that death "ends all things, and takes away life from every sentient being." In the same verse, he uses the word "extinction" as a synonym for the word "death."

---

138 *Ibid.*
139 *Ibid.*
140 Froom, *op. cit.*, 917–918.
141 Moyer, *op. cit.*, 18.

In *1 Disputations* 64:8, Arnobius says that Christ "was sent by the only [true] King ... to bring to you the immortality which you believe that you [already] possess, relying on the assertions of a few men" (i.e., the Greek philosophers, such as Plato, etc.). Clearly, Arnobius is not saying that **he** believes that his readers "[already] possess" immortality. On the contrary, it is his belief that immortality must be **brought** to them, and that Christ has done that. A few verses later (in *1 Disputations* 65:1), he says this "ungrateful and impious age" (referring to the pagan generation in which he lived) is "prepared for its own **destruction** by its extraordinary obstinacy." Later in that same chapter, he says Christ "told His enemies ... what must be done that they might escape **destruction** and **obtain** an immortality which they knew not" of (*1 Disputations* 65:13). And, in the next verse after that (*1 Disputations* 65:14), he says "that in no other way" than believing in Christ "could they avoid the danger of **death**."

In *2 Disputations* 1:8, Arnobius tells his pagan readers that Christ "prepared for you a path to ... the immortality for which you long"— but why would they "long" for something they already possessed by nature?

In *2 Disputations* 7:17, Arnobius reminds his pagan readers that "the soul ... is said by you to be immortal"—but he would not have needed to include the words "said by you to be" if he had believed the soul to be immortal, as he states that they did.

2 Disputations 14 is a comparison of Arnobius' own (Christian) doctrine of "hell" (v. 1) with Plato's (Greek philosophical) doctrine of "the immortality of the soul" (v. 1). Among other points made in this chapter are the following: Christians speak of "fires which cannot be quenched" (v. 1), while Plato says that "the soul is immortal" (v. 3); and Christians believe that the souls of the wicked are "annihilated" and "pass away vainly in everlasting destruction" (v. 7), while Plato "thought it inhuman cruelty to condemn souls to death" (v. 6). Arnobius concludes by expounding what he refers to as "Christ's teaching" (v. 8): that souls "perish if they have not known God" but

---

are "delivered from death if they have given heed to" Him (v. 8) and by stating that "man's real death ... leaves nothing behind" (v. 9) because "souls which know not God shall be consumed in ... fire" (v. 10). In the first verse of the next chapter (*2 Disputations* 15:1), Arnobius describes the "opinion ... that souls are immortal" as "extravagant."

In *2 Disputations* 16:3–5, Arnobius asks, "Will you lay aside your habitual arrogance, O men, who claim God as your Father, and maintain that you are immortal, just as He is? Will you inquire, examine, search what you are yourselves, whose you are, of what parentage you are supposed to be, what you do in the world, in what way you are born, how you leap to life? Will you, laying aside all partiality, consider in the silence of your thoughts that we are creatures either quite like the rest, or separated by no great difference?" He answers his own question three chapters later: "If men either knew themselves thoroughly, or had the slightest knowledge of God, they would never claim as their own a divine and immortal nature"; (*2 Disputations* 19:1). In *2 Disputations* 18:3, he says, "If the soul had in itself the knowledge which it is fitting that a race should have indeed which is divine and immortal, all men would from the first know everything"; which obviously is not the case since human beings keep learning new things as they go through life, and the entire "race" of human beings keeps learning new things as time passes. Similarly, in a lengthy discussion of the same subject, Arnobius states that "It has been believed that the souls of men are divine, and therefore immortal," and goes on to suggest that this idea "has been rashly believed and taken for granted" (*2 Disputations* 22:2)—and proceeds with an exhausting list of questions designed to disprove it.

Again, in *2 Disputations* 24:3, Arnobius portrays himself as asking Plato a question, beginning with the words, "**if** you are really assured that the souls of men are immortal" (implying that such a belief is Plato's, **not** his own), and in *2 Disputations* 25:2, he follows up this question with another, beginning with, "**Is** ... the ... soul ... immortal" (again, implying a negative answer).

Chapters 26–36 of *2 Disputations* contain numerous references to the subject of human immortality. *2 Disputations* 26:6, referring to "souls" (26:5), says that "The same reasoning not only shows that they are not incorporeal, but **deprives them of** all **immortality** even, and refers them to the limits within which life is usually closed."[142] Three chapters later, Arnobius presents a moral argument against the doctrine of Natural Immortality, asking, "How shall he be overcome by any fear or dread (i.e., of God's judgment) who has been persuaded that he is immortal, just as the Supreme God Himself, and that no sentence (i.e., of death) can be pronounced upon him by God, seeing that there is the same immortality in both, and that the one immortal being cannot be troubled by the other, which is only its equal" (2 Disputations 29:7)?[143] The point of this argument is similar to that raised by Jesus when He said, "Fear not them which kill the body, but are not able to kill the soul: but rather fear him which is able to destroy both soul and body in hell." (Matthew 10:28) (This verse, of course, is another "favorite" of many Conditionalists!)

An important insight into the fact that a "debate" was in progress between Naturalists and Conditionalists in Arnobius' time is given in 2 Disputations 31:2–3: "Thence it is that among learned men, and men endowed with excellent abilities, there is strife as to the nature of the soul, and some say that it is subject to death, and cannot take upon itself the divine substance; while others maintain that it is immortal, and cannot sink under the power of death ... because, on the one hand, arguments present themselves to the one party by which it is found that the soul is capable of suffering, and perishable; and, on the other hand, are not lacking to their opponents, by which it is shown that the soul is divine and immortal."144 In the next chapter, Arnobius makes it clear where he stood in the debate, saying, "We have been taught by the greatest teacher (i.e., Jesus) that **souls are** set **not far from** the gaping jaws of **death**; that they can, nevertheless, **have their lives prolonged** by the favor and kindness of the Supreme Ruler **if** only they try and

---

[142] Roberts, *op. cit.*, vol. 6, 444.

[143] *Ibid,* 445.

[144] *Ibid,* 446.

make an effort to know Him—for the knowledge of Him is a kind of vital leaven and cement to bind together that which would otherwise fly apart" (*2 Disputations* 32:1).[145] In Chapter 33, addressing readers presumed to be Naturalists (as all pagan Greek philosophers were), he adds, "**You** think that, as soon as you pass away, freed from the bonds of your fleshly members, you will find wings with which you may rise to heaven.... **We** shun such presumption, and do not think that it is in our power" (*2 Disputations* 33:3–4).[146]

Toward the end of this discussion, Arnobius asks, "If souls are mortal..., how can they ... become immortal?" (*2 Disputations* 35:1). His own answer to this question is given in the next chapter, where he says that "Immortality is God's gift" by which He will "deign to confer eternal life upon souls" otherwise destined to "utter annihilation" (*2 Disputations* 36:3).[147] Much later in the book, this teaching is summed up in the statement, "The souls of men ... are **gifted** with immortality, **if** they rest their hope of so great a gift on God Supreme, who alone has power to grant such blessings, by putting away corruption" (*2 Disputations* 53:1).[148] And in Chapter 62, Arnobius adds, "None but the Almighty God can preserve souls; nor is there anyone besides who can give them length of days, and grant to them also a spirit which shall never die, except He who alone is immortal."[149]

In *2 Disputations* 63:1, Arnobius portrays his opponents as saying that he (Arnobius) teaches that "Christ was sent by God for this end, that He might **deliver** unhappy souls **from** ruin and **destruction**...."

In *2 Disputations* 64:13, Arnobius defends his belief that God **offers** eternal life to human beings, but does not **compel** them to receive it—a view that, it seems to me, it would be difficult for a

---

[145] *Ibid.*
[146] *Ibid.*
[147] *Ibid,* 447.
[148] Roberts, *op. cit.*, vol. 6, 454.
[149] *Ibid,* 457.

Naturalist to hold—by saying that "our salvation is not necessary to Him, so that He would gain anything or suffer any loss, if He either made us [immortal] or allowed us to be **annihilated** and **destroyed** by corruption." Since it is clear that he had previously taught that God **did not** "make" human beings immortal, it is equally clear that he here teaches that God **does** "allow" them to be "annihilated" and "destroyed."

Comparing the Christian doctrine of salvation with pagan beliefs about the differing powers of their various gods, Arnobius states that "It is the right of Christ alone to **give salvation** to souls, and **assign** them **everlasting life** ... souls can **receive** from no one **life** and salvation, except from Him to whom the Supreme Ruler gave this charge and duty. The Almighty Master of the world has determined that this should be the way of salvation—this the door, so to say, of **life**—by Him alone is there access to the light: nor may men either creep in or enter elsewhere, all other ways being shut up and secured by an impenetrable barrier. So, then,... by no efforts will you be able to **reach** the **prize** of **immortality**, unless by Christ's **gift** you have perceived what **constitutes** this very **immortality**, and have been **allowed** to **enter** on the **true life**" (*2 Disputations* 65:11–66:1).

In *2 Disputations* 72:7, speaking of "the Almighty and Supreme God" (*2 Disputations* 72:4), Arnobius asks, "Is not He **alone** uncreated, **immortal**, and everlasting?" Although he does not actually quote 1 Timothy 6:16 (a favorite verse of many modern Conditionalists), he certainly makes the same point as is made there: **only** God is immortal; therefore, human beings are **not** immortal.

From all of these references, it is abundantly clear that "Arnobius was a militant Conditionalist."[150]

---

[150] Froom, *op. cit.*, 919.

Chapter 5
The Question Answered

Previously, our topic for discussion was defined as follows: "What can we learn from the writings of the early Church Fathers as to the position(s) held in their times on the subject of human immortality? Specifically, we will want to see whether the Apostolic, Subapostolic, and Ante-Nicene Fathers of the first, second and third centuries held a view similar to the popular modern view, or one more similar to the Conditionalist view."

After defining the two views and labeling them, for convenience, as "Naturalism" and "Conditionalism," respectively, I have reviewed the lives and works of twelve Apostolic, seven Subapostolic, and eleven Ante-Nicene Fathers, whose writings span the period from AD 95 to sometime between AD 303 and 310. As I said earlier, we have not studied every Christian writer of the first three centuries, but we have studied every Christian writer of the first three centuries in whose works I was able to find any references to the subject of human immortality.

Each of the thirty writers has been classified as either Conditionalist or Naturalist. Now the time has come to ask: what have we learned from this exercise?

It seems to me that the first, and perhaps most important, thing we have learned is that in the early Church, just as in the present-day Church, there were true, sincere Christians of the two doctrinal persuasions we have been studying. We have also seen that there was frequently an energetic, at times even vituperative, "debate" going on between the representatives of the two positions. Nevertheless, it is important to note that all of this was taking place **within** the broader context of the universal Christian fellowship generally known at the time as the "Catholic" Church. This was **not** primarily an argument between Christians and non-Christians, nor was it a "fight" between orthodox Christians and heterodox cultists. It was, in fact, a doctrinal discussion between individuals, and among groups, **all** of whom were members of the same worldwide Body of Christ, the Christian Church.

The second, and next most important, thing we have learned is that, during the period under study, Conditionalism, and not (as it is today) Naturalism, was the more prevalent view of the writings of the Fathers of the Church. This fact can be demonstrated by a simple enumeration, as follows:

Conditionalists:	16 definite, 4 probable	total, 20
Naturalists:	8 definite, 1 probable	total, 9
Unclassified:		1

So Conditionalism was favored over Naturalism by approximately a 2/3 majority of the thirty Fathers we have been able to classify.

Another question worth asking is: was this a regional conflict? Were the Fathers in one geographical area more inclined to Conditionalism, and the Fathers in another more inclined to Naturalism? The following chart will illustrate the surprising answer to this question:

Region	Conditionalists	Naturalists
Asia	8 or 9	1
Europe	7	2
Africa	2 or 3	5
(Unknown)	2	1

When you come to the next paragraph, you will see the reason why there seems to have been such a predominance of Conditionalism in Asia, the continent from which Christianity originated. The "surprise" is to see the contrast between the predominance of Conditionalism in Europe, the continent which later became the "world headquarters" of Christianity, and the predominance of Naturalism in Africa, the continent on which Christianity later became virtually extinct. One would have thought it would have been the other way around! What the chart really shows is that both Conditionalists and Naturalists could be found in all three areas of the world that were influenced by Christianity in the early centuries. I do not believe it shows that geography, or regionalism, really played a very important role in the debate at that time.

It seems to me that a much more significant role was played by the passage of time. The chart below is constructed so as to illustrate the "progress" of the two doctrines over the period of time covered by the study. It lists each Church Father under the appropriate heading in chronological order from the time of the Apostles (at the top of the page) toward the time of the Council of Nicaea (at the bottom).

Conditionalists	Naturalists
Clement of Rome	
Writer(s) of *Odes of Solomon*	
Ignatius of Antioch	
Polycarp of Smyrna	
Papias of Hierapolis	
Writer(s) of *Didache*	
Quadratus of Athens	
"Mathetes"	
Clement of Corinth	
Barnabas of Alexandria	
Aristides of Athens	
Hermas of Rome	
Justin of Samaria	
Tatian of Assyria	
Theophilus of Antioch	
Melito of Sardis	
	Athenagoras of Athens
Polycrates of Ephesus	
Irenaeus of Lyons	
Clement of Alexandria (unclassified)	
	Tertullian of Carthage
	Hippolytus of Portus Romanus

	Writer(s) of *Pseudo-Clementines*
	Minucius Felix of Africa
	Origen of Alexandria
	Commodianus of Africa
	Cyprian of Carthage
Novatian of Rome	
	Gregory Thaumaturgus of Neocaesarea
Arnobius of Sicca	

Looked at this way, the "score" becomes:

Prior to the time of Clement of Alexandria—	18 Conditionalists, 1 Naturalist
After the time of Clement of Alexandria—	2 Conditionalists, 8 Naturalists

It is clear from this chart that Conditionalism was the original doctrine of the Early Church (AD 95–177), and that Naturalism was first introduced by Athenagoras of Athens, and popularized by Tertullian of Carthage, after whose time it rapidly became the predominant view, though there continued to be an outspoken minority of Conditionalists.

Now it becomes clearer why Conditionalism was so much stronger in Asia during the first three centuries than it was in Europe and Africa. Asia was the continent on which Christianity originated. The churches of Asia held more tenaciously to the original doctrine (Conditionalism) while the churches in Europe and Africa were progressively coming under the influence of the more recent doctrine (Naturalism).

Outside the defined scope of this book, but certainly within the pale of relevance to its topic, is the question of how the debate between proponents of the two doctrines proceeded **after** the Ecumenical Council of Nicaea (AD 325). Briefly, the answer to this question is that the debate continued, with a higher and higher percentage of the post-Nicene writers embracing Naturalism as the centuries passed. At no point was unanimity reached. Finally, in 1513, the Fifth Lateran Council of the Roman Catholic Church officially condemned Conditionalism as heresy. Even then, however, the debate did not end. Only four years later, Martin Luther broke with Roman Catholicism and began the movement known today as Protestantism. He, and many other early Protestant leaders, such as John Wycliffe, William Tyndale, John Milton, and John Darby, revived the ancient belief in Conditional Immortality. Other reformers were Naturalists. So, while the debate was ended in the Roman Catholic Church, by official decree, it quickly sprang up again in the Protestant churches, and continues (there) to this day. As I mentioned in the Introduction, some denominations have taken an official "stand" for one position or the other. Many other denominations have kept their doors open to Christians of either persuasion. The "debate" continues.

Chapter 6
Concluding Remarks

We have seen that there are two radically different opinions on the question of human immortality: we have come to know them as Naturalism and Conditionalism. We have also seen that throughout most of Christian history a "debate" has raged between proponents of the two positions. Furthermore, we have discovered that almost all of the Church Fathers who wrote before AD 200 were Conditionalists, and that most of those who wrote between then and 310 were Naturalists. We have concluded that Conditional Immortality was the original, and predominant, doctrine of the early Church.

At this point I think it would be wise to reiterate that I have **not** sought to "prove" the correctness or incorrectness of either doctrine. I have only sought to determine which view was more prevalent in the early Church. That is why I have quoted extensively from the writings of the early Church Fathers and have **not** quoted frequently from the Holy Scriptures. I am by no means trying to imply that the Bible has nothing to say on this subject: on the contrary, it has so much to say that a much, much longer book would be required to cover it all. Nor am I implying that what the Bible says is not important. Rather, it is my belief that whatever the Bible teaches on this subject is of absolute and decisive importance. But it was the stated purpose of this book to analyze the views of the early Church, and the Bible's comments are therefore outside the defined scope of the book.

Many of the authors who have written on this subject have felt very strongly one way or the other. But it might be asked, "If there were a simple, clear, Biblical answer to the question of whether immortality is 'natural' or 'conditional,' why has there been debate over it for the past eighteen centuries?" For one thing, during many of those centuries, most people have not had an opportunity to study the Bible for themselves. Majority vote, ecclesiastical decree, heated invective, and even persecution, and the threat of death, have been used as tools for "settling" this issue. For another, even today, many churches exclude potential members unless they accept a prepackaged answer imposed on their conscience by signing a denominational Statement of Faith, or the Symbol of Faith. If more churches would keep their doors open to Christians of either persuasion, and allow this subject to be studied and answered from the Scriptures, we would be more likely to see this question answered decisively in our lifetime.

It has come to my attention that the Orthodox Church holds to the Conditionalist position. Dr. Brian Keen, a colleague, has provided proof from Protopresbyter John Romanides, an Orthodox theologian, and His Eminence, Hierotheos, Metropolitan Episcopate of Nafpaktos.

Part II
Application

Chapter 1
Introduction

Sometime before World War I, a young Canadian farmer, en route from his home in Ontario to Vancouver, British Columbia, encountered an Advent Christian on the train, and lengthy discussion with this fellow-traveller convinced him of the truth of the Advent message. He became an Adventist "in spirit," but, since there were no Advent Christian churches in British Columbia, he and his growing family attended the United Church of Canada for many years, having occasional fellowship with other Advent Christians at Camp Nooksack, in northern Washington State. Eventually his thirteen children and dozens of grandchildren formed a rather significant "band" of Adventists in the area around Chilliwack, British Columbia. It became almost customary, during the 1940s, for the various pastors of the Advent Christian Church in Sumas, Washington, to visit these people and hold Bible studies and prayer meetings with them. They seldom attended services at the Sumas church itself, but were usually to be found at Camp Nooksack at camp meeting time. In the early 1950s it was decided to attempt to establish an Advent Christian Church in Chilliwack, and the church first appears in the *Advent Christian Manual* in the 1953 edition, reporting twenty-eight members, a Sunday School enrollment of sixty-four, and a W.H. &F.M.S.[151] membership of ten, and listing Rev. Alvin E. Lobb (son of the original farmer from Ontario) as the pastor. After Rev. Lobb retired (approximately 1956), the church was pastored by a series of talented young men whose services were secured with denominational help; none of them, however, succeeded in expanding the membership of the church much beyond the borders of the extended Lobb family. Total membership peaked at thirty-nine (as recorded in the *Manual* in 1959); then a long, slow process of decline began. The church's last appearance in the *Manual* was in 1974; not long after that, it was

---

[151] Woman's Home and Foreign Missions Society

decided to close the work; the building was sold, and the proceeds donated to the Western Washington Advent Christian Conference.

Another example of the Advent Christian Church planting effort is the work of Rev. Frank J. Davis in the Washington, DC, area. Rev. Davis, a veteran home missionary of many years' experience, came to the nation's capital in the summer of 1944, supported by action of the Advent Christian General Conference, with specific purpose of exploring the possibilities of starting an Advent Christian church in what he called "this great strategic center" in his report. The story is told in much greater detail than should be reproduced here in Hazel Grant Hill's book, *Frank and Susie*. Suffice it to say that the "net result" of Rev. Davis' efforts is that today there is an Advent Christian church in Chillum, Maryland, which is listed in the 1980 edition of the *A.C. Manual* as having seventy-one members, a Sunday School enrollment of sixty-seven, a W.H. & F.M.S. membership of eighteen, a Men's Fellowship with eight members, a Youth Fellowship with eleven, a full-time pastoral ministry, and a church plant and parsonage property with a combined value of $220,000.00!

What is the difference between these two stories? How many new AC churches have been started in the past thirty years? Why do some succeed and continue to minister in the 1980s, and why do others eventually close? These questions (and others related to them) will be the subject of this paper, through the Aurora College Pastor-in-Residence program by Rev. John H. Roller, pastor of The Village Church of Carpentersville, Illinois, itself a "church planting" work begun in the 1950s which, for many years, has been riding the line between being a church that will eventually succeed and being a church that will eventually close.

The author is also deeply interested in the possible future of another such work: that begun in Tallahassee, Florida, by Rev. Hugh K. Shepard and what Rev. Dr. J. Howard Shaw calls "a dedicated and talented group of Advent Christians"—people who had moved to "Florida's beautiful capital city" from other parts of the state during the 1960s and 1970s. I will be assuming the pastorate of that work, Lord willing, during the month of June 1984, just ten weeks from the time of the writing of this book.

Chapter 2
Information

Here is a chart showing all the Advent Christian churches which made their first appearance in the *Advent Christian Manual* in the 1953 through 1980 editions:

Name and Location of Church	Name of First Pastor	First Listing	Last Listing
Chilliwack, BC	Alvin Lobb	1953	1974
Valley, Arleta, CA	Austin Warriner	1953	
Orlando, FL	John Davis	1953	
Riverview, Jacksonville, FL	Gordon Wilson	1953	1974
Augusta, ME	Edwin Barton	1953	1977
Chillum. MD	Robert Peterson	1953	
Community, Charlotte, NC	Victor Harrison	1953	1953
Dunn, NC	Lee Stancil	1953	
Charleston, SC	Arthur Whittier	1953	
Clinch Valley, VA	Bernard Tiller	1953	1974
Wesley Chapel, Mustoe, VA	E.C. Rutherford	1953	1969
Coco, Elkview, WV	Raphael Cavender	1953	
Fairview, Spencer, WV	Ralph Carpenter	1953	1955
Dunbar, WV	Hayford Cavender	1953	
Mt. Hope, Walton, WV	Troy Good	1953	1961
Lawndale, CA	Edgar Coontz	1955	1974
Clearwater, FL	I.F. Barnes	1955	
Oak Park, FL	A.J. Griffin	1955	1957
Wewahitchka, FL	A.J. Griffin	1955	1957
Barbourville, KY	Clarence Withrow	1955	
Natchitoches, LA	Walter Randolph	1955	1969
Saint Louis, MO	Frank Davis	1955	
Margaretville, NY	William Bailey	1955	
Durham, NC	Harrison Pritchard	1955	
First, Four Oaks, NC	Lee Stancil	1955	
Garner, NC	Wade Massengill	1955	
Grace, Wlimington, NC	Douglas Browning	1955	1977
Grundy, VA	Frank Cyphers	1955	1965
Baker's Fork, WV	James Looney	1955	1977
Greenbrier Valley, WV	Pearl Schoolcraft	1955	
Fort Myers, FL	John Cargile	1957	
Pensacola, FL	William Doty	1957	1967

Name and Location of Church	Name of First Pastor	First Listing	Last Listing
Tallahassee, FL	(none)	1957	1959
West Palm Beach, FL	Joyce Thomas	1957	1963
Mt. Zion, Nahunta, GA	E.H. Morgan	1957	
Dexter, ME	Delmar Lee	1957	1963
Cleveland, OH	Wilfred Balser	1957	1961
Creston, OH	Leon McElhaney	1957	
Faith, Medford, OR	Frank Dupray	1957	1971
Welcome, Wilder, VT	Howard Brown	1957	1961
Middle Creek, Cedar Bluff, VA	Joe Hankins	1957	
Lynnwood, WA	Donald Keepers	1957	
Fayetteville, WV	W.H. Hankins	1957	1959
Princeton, WV	Orville Harper	1957	
Friendship, Jacksonville, FL	Clyde Shepard	1959	
Southside, Jacksonville, FL	C.J. Bunch	1959	1974
Pleasant Grove, Branford, FL	J.A. Quinn	1959	1963
Highlands, LaGrange, IL	Wilsey McKnight	1959	
Covington, KY	Frank Davis	1959	1961
Hope, Lenox, MA	Raymond Bowden	1959	
Sumter, SC	Linwood Rowe	1959	
Spokane, WA	Philip Larson	1959	1967
Anawalt, WV	Paris Gross	1959	1959
Corinee, WV	Carl Gross	1959	1963
Christ's Chapel, Gainesville, FL	A.C. Hett	1961	1974
Pineridge, Jacksonville, FL	Ralph Roberts	1961	1974
Memorial, Lake City, FL	Howard Nason	1961	
Lakeland, FL	Howard Nason	1961	
St. Petersburg, FL	Sam Rawls	1961	
First, Augusta, GA	William Stringfellow	1961	
Ebenezer, Baxley, GA	Robert Keepers	1961	1977
New Hope, Waycross, GA	Elbert Aldridge	1961	
Raybon, Nahunta, GA	Harold Aldridge	1961	
Stone Mountain, GA	J.E. Almond	1961	
Village, Carpentersville, IL	William Harris	1961	
Corbin, KY	Thomas Hall	1961	
Grants, NM	Richard Polk	1961	1977
Greensboro, NC	Harrison Pritchard	1961	
Hollandale, NC	Franklin Turnage	1961	
Northfield, OH	David Comer	1961	1961
Brier Creek, SC	Albert Krau	1961	1961
Hampton, VA	Roy Baldwin	1961	1977
Laurel Fork, Pond Gap, WV	Cary Summers	1961	
Birmingham, AL	John Owens	1963	

Name and Location of Church	Name of First Pastor	First Listing	Last Listing
26th Ave., Santa Cruz, CA	(none)	1963	1963
Gardiner, ME	Sidney Lovering	1963	1963
Buffalo, NC	John Church	1963	1965
Blessed Hope, Lenoir, NC	Murray Coffey	1963	1977
Southside, Fort Worth, TX	Julian Gornto	1963	1971
Rand, WV	Denver Scarbro	1963	1963
Albuquerque, NM	Hugh Shepard	1963	1969
Memphis, TN	Ed Moffit	1963	
Tulsa, OK	(none)	1963	1963
Mariposa, CA	Jack LaDieu	1965	1974
San Jose, CA	David Buckley	1965	1969
East Buffalo, Tampa, FL	Cornelius Haisten	1965	
Gallup, NM	Delmar Lee	1965	1977
Castle Hayne, NC	Sidney Batson	1965	
Meadowview, Jacksonville, NC	George Saunders	1965	1977
Unity, Four Oaks, NC	Atlas Blackman	1965	
A.C., Wilmington, NC	Howard Brown	1965	1967
Wilson Chapel, Stewart, OH	Russell Tuthill	1965	1977
Hale's Corners, Milwaukee, WI	(none)	1965	1965
Walnut Park, Gadsden, AL	Carl Gross	1967	
Neighborhood, Huntsville, AL	David O'Coin	1967	1977
Montville, CT	Clinton White	1967	1977
Daytona Beach, FL	Herman Duke	1967	1969
Miramar, Miami, FL	M.G. Butterfield	1967	
Oak Grove, Miami, FL	M.G. Butterfield	1967	
Perry, FL	Wilfred Snyder	1967	
Bible Band, Lenoir, NC	John Church	1967	1969
Clayton, NC	Ralph Strickland	1967	
Concord, NC	Bobby Brock	1967	
Maranatha, Jacksonville, FL	Larry Withrow	1969	1971
Mills Memorial, Willard, NC	George Lane	1969	
9th St., Wilmington, NC	Bruce Blake	1969	1969
Dayton, OH	John Brooks	1969	1969
Faith, Columbia, SC	Gordon Joines	1969	1974
First, Vidalia, GA	James Herndon	1971	
Alley's Bay, Beals, ME	Raymond Brown	1971	
Elkton, MD	Benjamin Ferguson	1971	
Putnam Lake, NY	Laura Gibbs	1971	
Union, Walton, WV	Dennie Schoolcraft	1971	
Williams Mountain, WV	Larry Schoolcraft	1971	
Hope, Melbourne, FL	David O'Coin	1974	
Mt. Pleasant, Clayton, NC	Thomas Wood	1974	

Name and Location of Church	Name of First Pastor	First Listing	Last Listing
Old Sparta, Tarboro, NC	Jim Ellis	1977	
Raleigh, NC	Mike Barbour	1977	
Glen St. Mary, FL	Frank Underhill	1980	
Calvary, Savannah, GA	J.B. Nunez	1980	
Himyar, KY	W.T. Hall	1980	
Harbinger, Whitefield, NH	Earl Waterman	1980	
Plaistow, NH	David Squire	1980	
New Hope, Del City, OK	John Barclay	1980	
Sandtown, Finch, ON	Robert Rathbun	1980	
Mission, Columbia, SC	Ronnie Robertson	1980	
Roanoke, VA	Harold Aldridge	1980	

The total number of church-planting efforts included in the above list is 127. Of these, 68 (54%) are still open, while 59 (46%) have closed. Actually, since the last 9 churches in the list were just started in 1980, it would be more accurate to say that the total is 118, of which 59 (50%) are still open, while 59 (50%) have closed.

Chapter 3
Interpretation

One hundred and eighteen new churches in a period of a quarter of a century! By 1980, half of them are still in operation and half have ceased to exist! What factors caused "success" in some cases and "failures" in others? A few "suggestions" were encountered and investigated on Tuesday, Wednesday, and Thursday of my week of research. Here are the results.

First, I investigated the "mortality" statistics themselves, much as a life insurance company would do with a population of humans. For each of the 118 churches, at each "age" level, I asked the question: will this church appear in the **next** edition of the *A.C. Manual*? The result is the following chart. (Of course, as the "age level" increases, there are fewer and fewer churches to work with, since the more recently established ones have not yet reached the higher age levels!)

Years Since First Manual Appearance	Yes	No	Mortality Rate
0	107	11	9.3%
2	95	11	10.4%
4	89	5	5.3%
6	83	3	3.5%
8	80	3	3.6%
10	69	4	5.5%
12	65	3	4.4%
14	54	3	5.2%
16	46	4	8.0%

This means, for example, that four years after a church has first been listed in the *Manual*, there is a 5.3% chance that it will **not** appear in the next edition, corresponding to a 94.7% chance that it **will**. As can be seen from the chart, a church's "best" years in terms of survival potential prove to be the sixth to eighth years after its first *Manual* appearance. At that point, there is only about a 1.8% chance that the church will close in any given year (= a 3.6% chance that it will close in the next two-year period). It would certainly be a good feeling for a struggling group of members to know there is a 98.2% probability their little church will remain open at least another year! But **then** what happens? Ten years after the church's first appearance in the *A.C. Manual*, the "mortality rate" rises to 5.5%, and remains between 4% and 8% from then on. Evidently there is some sort of 'critical phase" that these new churches go through, generally about nine or ten years after their first appearance in the *Manual*, which in some way predisposes the church to either a continued success or an eventual failure. My research was too limited to demonstrate conclusively what factors in the church's life during this "critical phase" are "good" (leading to continued success) or "bad" (leading to eventual failure), but one pair of examples from personal knowledge might suffice to illustrate (or suggest) at least one possible difference.

The church in Carpentersville, Illinois made its first appearance in the *A.C. Manual* in 1961, under the leadership of its first full-time pastor, Rev. William S. Harris. Nine years later (during the "critical phase") they had just completed an ambitious building program, constructing a sanctuary to seat 168 persons, though the current membership of the church was only 22! Many of the people who had put arduous effort into the building program took a "back seat" at this point in the church's history, expecting that the availability of the new sanctuary would combine with the Pastor, Rev. Harris' efforts to the community with the Gospel and would produce the expected growth. Indeed, the following year saw the membership rise to an all-time high of 45: and then Rev. Harris was struck with a cerebral hemorrhage and died. The church went into a "tailspin," membership dropping back to 23 by the time a new pastor was secured and a new edition of the *Manual* produced. Financial problems have plagued the congregation ever since, and at the time of this writing it still remains uncertain whether the church will eventually pull through these difficulties and succeed, or eventually succumb to the problems and close.

Meanwhile, the church in nearby LaGrange, Illinois, made its first appearance in the *A.C. Manual* in 1959, under the pastoral leadership of Rev. Wilsey McKnight. Nine years later (during the "critical phase"), they were undergoing the third in a series of six pastoral changes that virtually constituted the church's history from 1959 through 1981! Membership rose and fell with each edition of the *Manual*, varying from a low of thirty-two in 1967 to a high of fifty-nine in 1971 (at which time there was no pastor listed in the *Manual*). A brief interview with Mr. Ross Mays, a former member of the church, confirmed what I had already suspected based on the above statistics: the congregation was relying almost entirely on the efforts of the members of the laity rather than on the leadership of a dynamic, effective pastor. Indeed, I think it bears repeating that the church reached its all-time high membership at a time when they were without a pastor altogether! Eventually, the "critical phase" behind them, a building program took place, *one of the lay members of the congregation became the pastor* (!), and a period of growth began which will certainly be evidenced in the statistics to appear in the 1984 *Manual* and which probably bodes well for the eventual continued resounding success of this promising young congregation.

Admittedly, two examples are insufficient grounds on which to base a theory, but I would like to suggest at least the hypothesis that one factor contributing to the stability of a new congregation is the involvement of its laity, especially during the ninth and tenth years after the first mention of the church in the *A.C. Manual*, and, correspondingly, that one factor which may contribute to instability and eventual closure is undue dependence on pastoral leadership, especially during that same critical phase of the church's history.

Another "suggestion" I tried to investigate was the question of whether the new church was located in an urban/suburban area or in a rural area. This involved some amount of subjective judgment as to whether a church should be classified as "urban/suburban" or "rural"; perhaps this research could be done again in more depth at a later time. But, for now, this is what I found:

Urban/Suburban Churches: Total—50; Open—24 (48%); Closed—26 (52%)
Rural Churches: Total—68; Open—35 (51%); Closed—33 (49%)

Apparently, rural churches have about a 3 percent better chance of survival than urban/suburban churches. This figure, of course, is far too small to be significant. It must be said that my research provides no evidence that there is any difference in the survival potential of new churches between those planted in the cities and suburbs and those planted in the countryside. As an illustration, consider the comparative membership statistics of two churches that both make their first appearance in the 1961 edition of the *Advent Christian Manual*; Stone Mountain, Georgia and Laurel Fork, West Virginia.

Year	Stone Mountain, GA (suburban)	Laurel Fork, WV (rural)
1963	22	12
1965	26	15
1967	32	17
1969	34	16
1971	57	25
1974	76	19
1977	73	21
1980	112	22

Both of these churches must certainly be rated as "successful" based on the above membership statistics, especially when it is considered that Stone Mountain is located in the suburbs of the largest city in the South (Atlanta), and Laurel Fork is located in a town (Pond Gap, WV) with a 1980 census population of 100!

A similar comparison can be made between the efforts to start churches in Tulsa, Oklahoma (urban) and Rand, West Virginia (rural) in 1963, both of which appeared only in the 1963 edition of the *A.C. Manual* and were never heard from again.

Neither "success" nor "failure," it would seem, has anything to do with the <u>size</u> of the community in which the church-planting effort is located.

Does it make a difference how many other Advent Christian churches are located in the vicinity of the new church? This is what I call the "fellowship factor:" it would seem logical to say that a new congregation needs the frequent fellowship and support of other Advent Christians and Advent Christian churches in the area. To measure this factor, I first grouped all the churches that remained open in 1980 and separated them from all the churches that had closed by 1980; I then asked, for each church, the question, were there more than thirteen other Advent Christian churches in the same state in the edition of the *Manual* previous to the one in which this church makes its first appearance, or less than thirteen? Not surprisingly, this was the result:

Churches That Remained Open: More than 13—43; Less than 13—16
Churches That Later Closed: More than 13—39; Less than 13—20

To put it another way: if a new church was planted in a state that had more than 13 other A.C. churches in it at the time of planting, it had a 60% chance of surviving till 1980; if it was planted in a state that had fewer than 13 other churches in it at the time, it had a 44% chance. This 16% better survival rate for churches planted in areas with more than 13 other Advent Christian churches around is certainly a significant figure supporting the "fellowship factor" theory.

A similar, and perhaps even more significant, question to ask is: does it make any difference how much support the existing Advent Christian churches in a given state give to church-planting ministry? It would certainly seem sensible to say that the more support for home missions there is in a given state, the higher will be the percentage of new churches in that state that succeed! Is there any way to measure this factor? I set up a chart showing **how many** new churches were started in each state during the course of the period in question, and how many of those were "successes" and "failures." It turned out that considerably more than half of the 118 new churches in question were located in four states: Florida (24), North Carolina (22), West Virginia (14), and Georgia (7). These were the only states in which more than six church-planting attempts were made; in twenty-three other states, fewer than six attempts were made in the entire period under study. In the four states in which there was a high interest in church planting, a total of 67 new churches were started; 39 (58%) are still open, while only 28 (42%) have closed. In the other thirty-three states, in which there was less interest in church planting, a total of 51 new churches were started: only 20 (39%) are still open, while 31 (61%) have closed. The difference between being in Florida, North Carolina, West Virginia, or Georgia, and being in some other state, was a 19% better survival rate, probably the most significant statistic I found in my studies here: it indicates the importance of **denominational support** to the eventual success or failure of a new church-planting ministry!

Some attempt was made to trace the importance of the involvement of key leadership in the early stages of each church-planting attempt: hence the listing in the chart at the beginning of this section of the name of the first pastor shown in the *Advent Christian Manual* for each church in the list. However, this question was too broad to submit to numerical analysis and too extensive to research in the limited time allotted for this study. I would like to remark, however, that a data on this subject could not be considered complete without the mention of a few names of persons who contributed greatly to the establishment of more than one new Advent Christian church in the period under study.

One of these has already been mentioned: Rev. Frank Davis, who first had the "vision" of an Advent Christian church in the nation's capital in the mid-1940s. To read his biography (*Frank and Susie* by his daughter, Hazel Grant Hill) is to be literally overwhelmed with the impression of how much work one man-and-wife team can accomplish in a lifetime of dedicated service on the home missions field! Much of Rev. Davis' work lies prior to the scope of this paper, since he was most active in the 1930s and 1940s, but even in his "retirement" he appears in the list at the beginning of this data, as the first pastor of the "successful" church-planting effort in St. Louis, Missouri in 1955. Indeed, it may accurately be said that Rev. Davis will be recognized by history as the unsurpassed giant in the field of Advent Christian church planting in the twentieth century: the "Babe Ruth" of home missions work, no matter what great things may yet be accomplished by others in the next decades, should the Lord delay his coming.

Another "great" man in the field is the author of the preface to *Frank and Susie*, Rev. Richard C. Polk (1917–1981). Rev. Dick Polk was pastoring First A.C. Church, Lenoir, North Carolina, the fifth time it appeared in the *Manual*; Central A.C. Church, Clifton Forge, Virginia, the fourth time it appeared; First A.C. Church, Dunbar, West Virginia, the second time it appeared; the mission church in Grants, New Mexico, the first time, and the highly successful (and previously mentioned) Stone Mountain, Georgia, church the sixth time it appeared in the *Manual*. But perhaps his crowning achievement (so says his obituary in the *Advent Christian News*) was his taking charge of the new work in Tallahassee, Florida, **before** it appeared in the *A.C. Manual*, and only three months before his death (which came September 27, 1981, as a result of a rapidly growing cancer). Such courage and dedication is worthy of the emulation of any minister, young or old, on whose heart God may lay the burden for home missions' work that Rev. Polk had!

Tribute such as this should not be given only to the deceased. Among many other dedicated men whose contribution to church-planting work should be mentioned in a book such as this, I would like to single out one other who is still at work: Rev. Hugh K. Shepard, who will probably appear in the 1984 edition of the *A.C. Manual* as interim pastor at the church Rev. Dick Polk had hoped to work with in Tallahassee, Florida. But this is not Rev. Shepard's first experience with new church ministry! He is listed in the 1963 edition of the *Manual* as the first pastor of the Albuquerque, New Mexico, A.C. Church, and he served for many years as Director of the Department of Evangelism and Home Missions of the Advent Christian General

Conference. His involvement with the new congregation in Tallahassee also goes far beyond what will be shown in the 1984 Manual, as will be seen in the later chapter on "Application" toward the close of this book.

One more "suggestion" ought to be discussed in the search for factors that promote either success or failure in Advent Christian church-planting efforts of the last thirty years: it is a suggestion that was given to me by Ernie Lobb, and it relates to the stories in Chapter 1 about the churches in Chilliwack, British Columbia and Chillum, Maryland. Does it make any difference whether the membership of the new church primarily consists of members of one particular family, or of members of several different and "unrelated" families? The stories of Chillum and Chilliwack would seem to imply that it does: that "one-family" churches might have a lower chance of continuing success than "several-different-family" churches. In the time allotted for this research, I was unable to pursue the question to any greater depth than that reflected in the opening chapter. But I suspect that further research in this area might support the thesis that a new church ought to have a "core group" consisting of members of several different and unrelated families if it hopes to eventually succeed and become a thriving, growing body of believers.

Chapter 4

Application

Outside the stated scope of this section, but definitely within the range of the author's interest, is the story of how the above described factors in the life of a church-planting effort may affect the new work in Tallahassee, Florida, which I will be leaving Illinois to engage in just a few months from now.

In January 1980, Rev. Hugh K. Shepard, veteran pastor, church planter and home missionary, shortly after his third attempt at retirement, went to visit some friends in Tallahassee—former members of his church in Panama City, Florida—and, in conversation with them, discovered that a number of other Advent Christians from different parts of Florida were now living in the Tallahassee area. Immediately his church planter's heart conceived the idea of starting a new Advent Christian church there. For six months he and Mrs. Shepard made regular monthly visits to Tallahassee to meet with the Advent Christian people there and discuss with them the possibility of organizing the new work. Eventually it was decided to begin holding Sunday services, and Reverend Shepard assumed the role of interim pastor until a full-time minister could be found to coordinate the work.

No better man could have been found for the job than the man who, in January 1981, "was appointed as the Church Planter for (the) new mission" according to the headline article in the September 30, 1981 issue of the *A.C. News*: Rev. Richard C. Polk of Stone Mountain, Georgia. The rest of that article reads as follows:

> *"He was to have begun work in April (1981), but malignancy was discovered. After surgery, the surgeon assured him and the family that he had gotten it all and there should be no recurrence. The Tallahassee congregation reaffirmed their desire to have Rev. Polk come.*

In July (1981), Dick and Marion moved there and purchased a mobile home. During the weeks of his ministry, a number of new families were contacted and new faces were present at services every week. Just as a beautiful 4-acre property was being purchased for location for the mission, Pastor Polk was hospitalized again, in mid-August. X-rays showed the malignancy was in the lymph glands and spread rapidly. On September 21, he was moved to the J. Ralph Smith Health Center at the Advent Christian Village. Death came early the morning of September 27."

It is still "conventional wisdom" to assume that the Tallahassee work would be thriving and growing today if Reverend Polk had lived, though of course only the Lord really knows what "might" happen if things go differently than they actually do.

What **did** happen is that Reverend Shepard came back to serve a second term as interim pastor while the congregation and the Conference Home Missions Committee searched for another qualified individual to pick up where Reverend Richard Polk had unwillingly left off.

On October 4, 1981, the Advent Christian Church of Tallahassee held its first service at the beautiful location at 989 Maddox Road which Rev. Polk had worked so tirelessly to obtain on their behalf.

According to another article in the *A.C. News* –

"A half-dozen experienced men were contacted as prospective pastor, but none were ready to step into a brand new work. The months dragged on. The Mission Committee discussed the new two-year Church Planter Training Program, designed by the denominational Office of Church Expansion. It provided comprehensive training and supervision for men right out of college, as well as for men with pastoral experience.

Prayerfully, they asked about the availability of a 1982 Berkshire Christian College graduate.

In March 1982, the director of Church Expansion had enrolled the first person in the new Church Planter Training Program: Craig Wert, then a senior at Berkshire Christian College. Craig had the needed qualifications for this specialized ministry, and eagerly tackled the training responsibilities. He was recommended to the governing board of the Tallahassee work, and they invited him to come to Tallahassee the first of June 1982."

Craig and Rhonda dove into their new work enthusiastically, and much success was reported for several months in various items in the *A.C. News.* Typical among these are Craig's appearance on a local Christian radio station's *Pastor's Program* and the baptism of three candidates in the spring of 1983. However, the next item in the *News* is dated November 4, 1983, and reflects the fact that Craig left Tallahassee to assume a New England youth pastorate in August (1983) by simply stating, "Rev. Hugh Shepard is now serving as interim pastor at the Tallahassee Advent Christian Church." (For the third time, I might add!) And again the search began for a full-time pastor for the young church.

In October 1983, Dr. J. Howard Shaw, Executive Secretary of the South Georgia and Florida A.C. Conference and Chairman of the Conference Home Missions Committee, wrote a letter to a young man he had known while serving as pastor of the Advent Christian Church of the Highlands in LaGrange, Illinois (one of the "successful" church-planting efforts described earlier in the paper!), Rev. John H. Roller, Pastor of the Village Church of Carpentersville, Illinois, to inquire if he might be interested in considering the opportunity of coming to Tallahassee to continue the work begun under the leadership of Rev. Shepard, Rev. Polk, and Mr. Wert. The net result of that letter was that Rev. Roller came to Tallahassee the last week of February 1984 to candidate, and on March 11, 1984, was extended—and accepted—a call to the pastorate. Reverend Shepard is presently scheduled to conclude his "interim" service to the congregation on Easter Sunday (April 22), 1984, and Rev. Roller hopes to arrive in Florida with his family sometime during the month of June.

Based on the observations made in the paper and other similar observations about success and failure in church-planting ministry, Rev. Roller has the following personal goals for ministry in Tallahassee. (It is, of course, understood that these goals are, first of all, highly tentative, depending to a large extent on additional findings that will be made after my arrival in Florida, and secondly, entirely personal, in no way having been considered or approved by the Tallahassee congregation or the Conference Home Missions Committee.)

First, after my arrival in Tallahassee later this spring, I hope to engage in a "quiet" phase of ministry for at least six months to a year, making little attempt to effect changes in the present structure and program of the church and essentially trying to find a "niche" for myself as pastor, and for my family, **within** that structure and program, rather than "imposing" myself and my ideas on the congregation from the outside. (For this concept, I am indebted to the example of Rev. Jim Crouse, of Baraboo, Wisconsin, who, I was told by an adoring member of his church, "did nothing" by way of changing the prevailing mood of the church "until he had been here a year and knew us well enough to change us without offending us." I believe his concept and pattern is worthy imitation!...)

Then, after I know the ropes, I hope to use my position as their Pastor to encourage the members of the congregation to discover and develop their own spiritual gifts in a manner described in *Ephesians* 4:11ff:

> *"And he gave some apostles, and some prophets, and some evangelists, and some **pastors and teachers**, for the **building up** of*

*the **saints** for the work of service, in order to build up the body of Christ...."*

To me, this verse implies that it is a pastor-teacher's job **not** to do "the work of service ("ministry")" **himself**, but rather, to "**build up**" the **lay** members of the congregation, that **they** might be capable of "doing the work." Not only is this concept Biblical, but, in addition, as we have seen in this section, it is characteristic of **growing** young churches that they rely heavily on **lay** (rather than "professional") ministry in the critical phase of their life, which will come, for the Tallahassee work, approximately 1993–1994 if the Lord delays his return that long.

As far as a building program is concerned, it is my belief that it is dangerous for a church to invest too much (too much time, too much energy, too much money) too soon (in the early years of its history, when finances are least stable) in the project of erecting a sanctuary, usually at great expense to the local budget as well as heavy involvement in denominational subsidy and, worse yet, deficit spending with the "generous" help of secular financial institutions. (In other words, mortgage loans!) I think it would be safer for the folks in Tallahassee to continue to meet in their present beautiful facility while **gradually** (slowly!) working on acquiring a more permanent one. They might, for example, first seek a piece of land more visible from a nearby highway, purchase it with the help of a capital funds drive, and put up a sign reading something like, FUTURE SITE OF THE ADVENT CHRISTIAN CHURCH OF TALLAHASSEE (now meeting at 989 Maddox Road). Then, a temporary meeting structure might be erected on that land—perhaps a tent like that at Riverwoods Christian Center (formerly known as Camp Rude) in St. Charles, Illinois, or perhaps a double-wide mobile home hollowed out to form a temporary sanctuary. Later, more permanent facilities can be erected, perhaps piece by piece, over an extended period of time, until eventually a completed house of worship stands in a good location, fully paid for, and housing a congregation that has grown with it to the point where it is sized appropriately for the needs of the group. This project may take longer than one man's ministry, but it is a project that will keep financial expenditure within the congregation's reach and will, at the same time, keep the church continually in the eyes of the community as a growing, progressing organism with always something to look forward to as well as something usable "in hand" at the moment. It is a process that can continue until Jesus comes, if necessary, without ever being a "burden" to the people involved in it, or to those supporting them with prayer and advice.

Eventually, I would hope that the Tallahassee congregation will be able to continue indefinitely in a program of reaching the community for Christ in the name of the Advent Christian Church, with dedicated and gifted lay people doing the work under godly, progressive leadership, the finest the denomination will have to offer. I do not see myself as being the pastor there by the time that goal is achieved. Like Frank Davis and Dick Polk before me, I am aware that I have a personal "heart" and "burden" for the works that are new and struggling. Right now that burden draws me to the capital of the nation's fastest growing state, but I am sure at some point in the future, Lord willing, the same burden will draw me somewhere else. I hope, though, that the ideas contained in this section may later prove to be my "legacy" to this promising young church of which I will soon be the pastor. And I know that what I learn in Tallahassee will help me do an even better job of church planting wherever it is that I may go after there.

Part III
Consequences

This is a case study regarding the attempts to grow by the Advent Christian Church, who are the chief advocates of conditional immortality. This case study starts when the Ecclesia comes to the Earth rather than when the Adventist movement or the Advent Christian denomination commenced. The Adventist movement was a spontaneous outpouring of Christians discovering a number of realities of the Truth and the Ecclesia. One of the dominant realities was that there was a Second Advent, hence the name Advent Christian Church.

Any business, enterprise, or profession must look at the history of how it commenced and how it develops over time. Your enterprise may have lasted centuries, such as the Ecclesia. There must be an assessment of why your business, enterprise, or profession was needed. If you are an entrepreneur, you will need to assess why and where your competitors have come from, since there is a need to build on their history, whether you like it or not.

We should research as many successful examples as are appropriate to ensure, not only a successful enterprise, but the potential for immortality.

Are you aware that there are enterprises that have existed for centuries? Do you realize that the Church has existed for almost 2,000 years— teaching that Jesus is the Truth and the only source of immortality?

We can analyse sources of church growth that have attained phenomenal success. We will evaluate:

- ❖ a successful church planter named Nicholas;
- ❖ a phenomenal community that literally built a cathedral in Eagle River, Alaska;

❖ an example of perseverance in an extremely hostile environment; and
❖ how these relate through reinvigorating our businesses and enterprises.

Nicholas

Nicholas is an example of a successful entrepreneur who worked within an ethos that he did not understand initially. He didn't even know the language. The numbers prove that the time he took to learn the language was invaluable—he actually went to an elementary school and stood at the back of a class. Let us see how he did.

Nicholas was sent to Japan as a church planter in order to share Christ with Japanese. He was mentored by Innocent who told him to concentrate on learning the Japanese language, history, and culture. Nicholas arrived in Hakodate, Japan, in 1861.[152] Can you imagine starting to do any job when you have absolutely no knowledge of the language or anything about the community in which you are going to work as an entrepreneur?

Nicholas started small, gathering those Japanese who responded to the Good News of Jesus as the Truth initially in Hakodate. The first step was establishing a simple chapel. Eventually, the Church of the Resurrection was built in 1916.[153] As your business or enterprise grows it is possible to build for necessary expansion. In this case, the capital of Japan moved to Tokyo, so Nicholas made Tokyo the centre of his mission. When circumstances change, it is necessary for entrepreneurs to react to these changes. If a move is appropriate, we move.

---

[152] Michael Van Remortel and Dr. Peter Chang (ed.), *Saint Nikolai and the Orthodox Mission in Japan: A Collection of Writings by an International Group of Scholars about St. Nikolai, His Disciples, and the Mission*, Point Reyes Station: Divine Ascent Press, 2003, 5–7.
[153] Chang, *Mission*, 39–44.

Nicholas encouraged the newly Illuminated to seek the Truth's Will, encouraging them to consider becoming catechists. The catechist is the person who trains catechumens in understanding the Good News.

Many catechists continued to work in their regular job or profession. If the catechist was transferred to another community, he or she would simply commence the establishment of a new mission. Special training and assistance were available to the catechists and catechumens. Initially, the catechist's home or office could be utilized as the mission's home. As the mission grew, the catechists would secure a location for the mission's meeting house. This would allow a facility that could provide numerous training opportunities for several catechumens who may have need for more or less training to prepare them for Illumination.

Eventually, as the catechists recognized that there was further growth, there would be an application to establish a chapel. This chapel could be a room in a larger meeting house, or a stand-alone temporary building. If possible all of the development could take place on one appropriate property that had potential for growth to build a cathedral. At this time, some of the catechists could be considering a call to the ministry as a deacon (deacons in the Orthodox Church are paid a salary). In this case the catechist would apply for training at the theological seminary through the appropriate authorization of the senior pastor (Orthodox refer to them as the episcopate). Some catechists might continue throughout their lives in this calling, since Orthodox regard catechists as an appropriate ministry for entrepreneurs, professionals, or people who work.

The goal for all catechists was the eventual establishment of a parish church. A parish would require an extensive building that could accommodate the future growth of the community. For example, if a community has a population of 5,000 but had a potential of 500,000, the parish church should be built for perhaps 10,000 yet have the acreage to eventually expand the parish church. This was not always possible, since many of the Church membership (called Theanthropic

Communities in the Orthodox Church) may have only 1,000 versus the 5,000 in the community.

According to Dr. Brian Keen, a parish church would require a minimum of either: three presbyters (pastors, perhaps an associate pastor and assistant pastors) and two deacons (primarily responsible for social service work), or two presbyters and three deacons. This would depend on the needs of the parish church and the strength of the catechumen training by catechists.

The goal for all of the Illuminated is the establishment of a cathedral. This requires a cathedral complex. Among the facilities required for a cathedral complex are: a temple with an appropriate staff of numerous presbyters, deacons, catechists; a theological seminary requiring a dean, presided over by the episcopate; buildings containing meeting rooms; apartments for visitors and staff and families requiring overnight rest; and ecclesiastical offices (e.g. media facilities).

The closest example of a cathedral complex available for us to view is the Christ Cathedral (formerly the Crystal Cathedral) complex with numerous buildings.[154]

Since Nicholas recognized the benefits of the indigenous population, he encouraged the newly Illuminated to consider ministry. In fact, the first Japanese person who came to Illumination worked with Nicholas throughout his life. They worked on translating all of the necessary works, such as the Scriptures, to build up the mission as the Body of Christ. The vast majority of the ministry personnel were Japanese. Nicholas even saw himself as Japanese when a war broke out between Russia and Japan.

---

[154] For a thorough evaluation of every building, refer to www.christcathedralcalifornia.org.

Nicholas made extensive plans for a proper cathedral complex in Tokyo. There were plans designed in 1891 as an Art Print of the Holy Resurrection Cathedral.[155] Unfortunately, as you can see below only half of the cathedral complex was completed.

This is what the Holy Resurrection Cathedral looked like when it was constructed in 1891. The present building is essentially the same as we see here.

Nicholas established the following over the forty-eight years of church planting: two cathedrals, seven parish churches, 276 chapels, and 175 meeting houses. He personally ordained thirty-four presbyters (pastors), eight deacons, and 115 catechists. The result was 34,110 people who came to a knowledge of Jesus Christ as the Truth.[156] This is a wonderful success story. Can you imagine if you, as an entrepreneur, had an enterprise with two box stores, seven large

---

[155] Contribution by Professor Kennosuke Nakamura, "St. Nikolai's Spirituality and Evangelical Vision," cited in Chang, *Mission*, 89.

[156] Contribution by Mitsuo Naganawa, "Archbishop Nikolai Kasatkin: A Russian Evangelist in Japan," cited in Chang, *Mission*, 122.

facilities, 276 smaller facilities, and 175 offices? Can you imagine if an entrepreneur had over 30,000 regular customers or clients?

This is the answer to the quandary that I presented in Section II. We must always look for successful enterprises in our particular field. It isn't necessary to follow their example slavishly, yet we must consider that success has been achieved. This is particularly relevant when we see success over an extended period of time, as you saw in my examples of failed churches (or enterprises) being approximately 50 percent of the church planting.

Community

We will now look at an example of a church planter who went to Alaska to establish a community based upon the example of L'Abri[157] Fellowship. Harold and Barbara Dunaway moved to Alaska and settled in Eagle River. Their Ecclesiastical Community has been documented in *Community of Grace: An Orthodox Christian Year in Alaska* by Mary Alice Cook. The results are phenomenal. Let us consider their entrepreneurship and how they became successful.

The community started with a large house called the Big House, Maranatha North. Eventually this community became Orthodox as a member of the Evangelical Orthodox Church. They sought how Christ established His Church, and implemented the system they discovered through various sources from the Ecclesia. This community started to grow as the denomination grew.

The community became totally self-sustaining through encouraging all of the laity to find their individual calling from Christ. For example, Robin is an iconographer with a studio in the community cathedral.

---

[157] L'Abri means shelter. For more information about the L'Abri Fellowship movement go to: http://www.labri.org.

The cathedral building was built by the community for the community. There is a cemetery and numerous facilities that assist the Community in meeting every conceivable problem.

The community attracted the famous missionary Archimandrite Lazarus to live there. Upon his repose he is now remembered as "Archimandrite Lazarus of Eagle River, Alaska."[158]

There are tremendous opportunities for the community to come together. There is an annual salmon run where everyone participates, from the youngest to the oldest, in every conceivable task for the benefit of the community.

One of the most important services in this community is the vesper service on Forgiveness Sunday (the Sunday prior to Great Lent), where everyone in the community asks for and receives forgiveness from every other member of the community. This has significantly impacted the community living the Law of Love.

This an exemplary community that can be duplicated as the Church grows from a mission to a parish until it becomes a cathedral complex, like Eagle River. Eagle River has a cathedral complex for the Antiochian Diocese of Eagle River and the Northwest, which includes Alaska, Alberta, British Columbia, Idaho, Oregon, Saskatchewan, Utah, and Washington.

Perseverance

We will now look at one of the senior pastors who lived a life of perseverance. His name was Luke, and this is based upon the book, *The Blessed Surgeon: The Life of Saint Luke Archbishop of Simferopol*. This is a man name Luke who was a world-famous

---

[158] Saint Herman Brotherhood, *Saint Herman Calendar* 2015, Platina: St. Herman of Alaska Brotherhood, 2015, November 14/27, 100

pioneer in the field of medical surgery. Throughout his life, Luke was a much sought-out surgeon. Unfortunately, he refused to accept the stupidity of the Soviet Union in attacking and arresting Orthodox members for their faith in Christ. Luke was outspoken with reference to his faith, which meant that an icon was always present when he operated on patients.

Luke became a doctor prior to the Russian Revolution. He married Anna who was a nurse. They had two children, a son Michael born in 1907 and a daughter Helen born in 1908.

When the Bolshevik Revolution started there were shortages of food and violence became a normal situation—even near the hospital. There were times when bullets came even into the operating room with medical staff being struck on occasion. The stress of the revolution caused the death of Anna at the age of 38! He was now a widower with two young children. Christ intervened and He told Luke to marry an unknown nurse named Sophia. Sophia listened to Luke and agreed that this was Christ's Will, so she became the mother of Michael and Helen.

Luke was soon arrested after he was ordered to remove the icon from the operating room. While Luke was awaiting trial, the wife of one of the Communist Party members required surgery and demanded that Luke perform this surgery. Luke insisted that the icon be returned to the operating room. It was and the surgery was successful.

With the numerous arrests of episcopates and presbyters by the militant atheists, it was decided that Luke should be ordained a presbyter. He was well known for his faith in Christ and his defence of the faith.

The militant atheists found an excuse for arresting Luke based on their "expert" opinion about how soldiers in the Red Army had been mistreated. It turned out that the "worms" that the "experts" wanted washed off were, in fact, larvae that were healing the soldiers. Luke cited his credentials as a medical professional graduating from one of the most prestigious medical schools—University of St. Vladimir in Kiev. In spite of these scientific proofs, Luke and his colleagues were found guilty. Upon appeal, they were set free.

The Soviet Union started a "Living Church" to overthrow the Orthodox Church of Russia by seizing Her property. Luke quickly came to the defence of the Orthodox. As a presbyter, Luke was able to refute the claims of the proponents of the "Living Church" with the Orthodox people.

The city of Tashkent required an episcopate. Luke was then ordained to the episcopacy knowing that this would mean more problems from the Soviet authorities through their attacks.

Soon Luke was arrested and tortured by the GPU (short for State Political Directorate). Luke was convicted of being a political criminal and sent to Moscow. The cells in the prison had 140 prisoners, which were designed for twenty-five prisoners. Luke cared for others, which positively influenced many fellow prisoners.

When Luke was exiled to Yeniseisk, he went to the chief physician of the hospital and offered his services. The chief physician knew of Luke's reputation as an exceptional surgeon. Luke was asked to perform several complicated operations. Soon there was a three-month waiting list from patients wishing to see Luke. This became an irritant to the local Soviet officials. When Luke openly served and ordained a presbyter at the Church of the Transfiguration in Yeniseisk, they sent him to another exile. This time he was sent to Turukhansk.

Luke encouraged the Orthodox faithful in Turukhansk and performed surgery at the local hospital. The GPU officer forbade Luke from blessing and praying for patients. Luke refused, so the GPU director exiled Luke to the Arctic Ocean. Prior to Luke's travelling, he returned to the hospital to perform surgery. Patients cried as the police escorted Luke to his exile.

Luke courageously arrived in the Arctic, chastising the owner of a house for not receiving an episcopate in the correct fashion. The escort police officer was quite taken with Luke's power. The Lord Jesus Christ told Luke that he would be returning to Turukhansk within a month.

In the meantime, one of the citizens of Turukhansk had died due to Luke's absence. Without Luke's expertise the citizen had died, so the people armed themselves with pitchforks and axes and threatened the destruction of the GPU and the council building. The authorities ordered Luke back.

Despite the continuous torture, Luke returned from the Arctic exile in good spirits. He returned to working in the local hospital. The GPU director went to visit Luke in the hospital. A group of people came making the gesture requesting Luke's episcopal blessing. Luke was happy to bless all of the people. The GPU director had to pretend that he didn't see this episode.

Luke missed his son, daughter, and wife, but Luke trusted Christ. Can you imagine how the children would react hearing about numerous episcopates and presbyters being executed or starving to death? As an entrepreneur, we never experience this type of ridicule. Maybe our families ridicule us for our ideas, but never do we have to worry about being exiled from our family.

After eight months, Luke's exile in Turukhansk ended. Christ communicated with Luke to assure him of His Love for His Episcopate. This is something to a greater or lesser degree, as entrepreneurs, we can relate to. The Truth, Who is Christ, Loves us as entrepreneurs for resolving problems and creating wealth for many.

Upon receiving his freedom, he met with another episcopate and a monastic. The monastic had lost his sight in one eye. Luke contacted the ophthalmological department of the local hospital requesting permission to operate. A group of doctors requested permission to observe the operation. Luke was happy to teach these doctors how he performed this surgery. Luke showed them step-by-step with a painless and almost bloodless operation. This was performed prior to laser surgery.

Luke was arrested a second time and exiled. Essentially the same type of situations developed. The people needed his tremendous skill as a surgeon who continued to heal all people, both physically and spiritually. He insisted on wearing his cassock and having an icon as he performed surgery. During his second exile he produced *Essays on the Surgery of Pyogenic Infections*, published in 1934.

Luke was arrested and exiled a third time. The unique aspect of this time was that Luke went on a hunger strike. There were the usual beatings and tortures. His daughter, Helen, was allowed to visit him. Helen was allowed to speak to her father through a hole in an iron door.

Luke was exiled during what the Russian (not the Soviets) call the Great Patriotic War, which we in North America call World War II. Despite living in poverty and near starvation, Luke continued to work at a local hospital and revising *Essays on the Surgery of Pyogenic Infections*. He researched new German, French, and English articles relating to surgery for pyogenic infections. This is exactly how we, as entrepreneurs, react to adversity. We constantly seek the Truth to improve our knowledge of how to resolve all problems better.

Luke wrote a second edition of *Essays on the Surgery of Pyogenic Infections* in 1943. In 1944 he published *Late Resections of Infected Gun-shot Wounds in Joints*. He received the prestigious Stalin Award first degree for these two books.

In 1947, Luke published *Spirit, Soul, Body* to offer illumination to those who had fallen away from the Orthodox faith. He attacked the atheistic propaganda about the contradictions between science and Christianity. He would know since he was both an episcopate and a medical surgeon. He healed people holistically. As entrepreneurs, we need to be aware that we must deal with all stakeholders in a holistic way.

Luke was transferred to Simferopol, Crimea, to oversee the pastoral work. He was seventy years of age when he evaluated the situation. He found that there were numerous items lacking from the sixty-eight churches for which he was responsible. There was a lack of clergy, while the few serving were poor examples to others. He challenged all to live for Christ. He insisted on catechumens training to assure that all in the churches knew their faith in Christ correctly. He disciplined those who failed to be Disciples of Christ. Clergy were trained in all of the correct methods of counselling and taking care of the poor. He wrote and gave numerous sermons throughout Simferopol.

In addition, Luke worked as a consultant to the Simferopol Hospital. He regularly attended physicians' meetings listening to reports and speeches. He offered advice for improving surgical techniques. Of course, he stood out because he continued to wear his episcopal vestments.

Luke passed away on June 11, 1961.

Luke had personally done the following:

- ❖ Graduated from the medical department of the University of Kiev.
- ❖ From 1910 to 1916 he was director of the hospital in the city of Pereslavl-Zalesskiy.
- ❖ In 1917 he became director-professor and surgeon in Tashkent.
- ❖ In 1920 he became professor of anatomy and interventional surgery at the University of Tashkent.
- ❖ From 1920 to 1930 he was exiled to Siberia.
- ❖ From 1940 to 1945 he was chief surgeon (Great Patriotic War).
- ❖ He was awarded the state award of the USSR in 1946 for his work as surgeon and doctor.

❖ He authored more than thirty books, including *Surgery of Pyogenic Infections* in 1934 and *Pyogenesis in Machine Wounds of Joints* in 1944. He received the Stalin award for all of these books.

Luke is a wonderful example for all of us who are entrepreneurs. This is someone who overcame extreme persecution, yet continued to be an exemplary surgeon and specialist in the medical profession. He did everything he could to resolve medical problems. In addition, he was an exemplary episcopate during a time of horrific persecution, when many of his colleagues were martyred.

Reinvigorate

The challenge of reinvigorating a business, enterprise, or profession must first be to look at the historical story in order to ascertain whether there are seasonal challenges that have occurred over time, or whether there are reasons that can rectify the problems. There are reasons for the start and the ending of a profession, enterprise, or business. Only the Ecclesia lasts forever. Immortality is conditional as we have learned.

The Truth has the answer to immortality, whether for an individual as an entrepreneur, or as a business, enterprise, or profession.

The first reality that must be determined is what the size of an enterprise, profession, or business is in reality. Let us look at objective standards established by the Canadian accounting profession to determine the size.

❖ A micro-sized enterprise is one that has annual revenues of less than $3,000,000 per annum.
❖ A small enterprise is one that has annual revenues of less than $15,000,000 per annum.

❖ A medium size enterprise has annual revenues of less than $75,000,000 per annum.

How do you measure up in reality?

Based on the research presented, your enterprise can learn how to reinvigorate if you really desire immortality.

Now that you know what a micro-sized enterprise is, you can plan to establish appropriately. My experience shows that you must be careful how fast you grow. It is also important for all of us to be totally committed to the Truth. We have seen that when Nicholas started, he commenced by utilizing catechists to train catechumens. Community was essential for Nicholas and at Eagle River. We all must realize that community is an important component.

As our enterprise grows into a small enterprise, we can see that both the community and Nicholas were able to continue to grow. Luke was able to adapt to every situation thrown at him by the militant atheists in the Soviet Union. The facilities need to be appropriate for the small-sized enterprises.

When we grow into a medium enterprise, we can see that the community grew into their role and are an example to our enterprise if we stay in one community. There is nothing wrong with being an enterprise that exists only in one location. For example, what exists in Oxford aside from Oxford University? Nicholas had objective standards for what size facilities were necessary for the numerous communities in which they were working. The medium-sized facility would be the parish church. If you, as an entrepreneur, are going to have numerous communities and various sizes of facilities, remember Nicholas who was very successful.

When we grow into a large enterprise, we can look to both community and Nicholas to maintain and continuously grow. Nicholas's legacy in Japan is still alive and well for over a century of existence. His Communities and their facilities continue to exist despite tremendous challenges, especially during World War II. The Community of Eagle River has existed for over thirty-five years.

What is remarkable about Luke is that while the Church of Russia has been active for over a millennium (988 to 1988), he ministered during a time of extreme hatred by atheists (so much for the song "Imagine") who slaughtered all who had faith in any god or God.

You will never know, unless you are in Christian ministry, if your enterprise will last for eternity. You have a choice. You can be immortal, and your enterprise can be immortal.

This is my personal invitation to learn about Jesus Who is the source of immortality.

Bibliography

__The Holy Bible__. London, Her Majesty's Printer, 1611.

An Association of Believers. *Good Tidings*. Boston: 1885.

+Jonah, Metropolitan of Washington (Publisher). *Saint Nikolai and the Orthodox Mission in Japan*: *A Collection of Writings by an International Group of Scholars about St. Nikolai, His Disciples, and the Mission*. Point Reyes Station: Divine Ascent Press, 2003.

Atkinson, Basil. *Life and Immortality*. Taunton: Phoenix Press, undated.

Barton, Freeman. *Heaven, Hell and Hades*. Charlotte: Advent Christian General Conference, 1981.

Barton, Freeman. *Our Destiny We Know*. Charlotte: Venture Books, 1996.

Brandyberry, James. *The Development of the Doctrine of Immortality from the Apostolic Fathers to Augustine in Henceforth*, Volume XII, Number 1, 1983.

Brauer, Jerald. *The Westminster Dictionary of Church History*. Philadelphia: Westminster Press, 1971.

Cargile, John A. *True Theology*. Boston: Advent Christian Publications, 1887.

Charlesworth, James H. (editor). *The Old Testament Pseudepigrapha*, two volumes. New York: Doubleday, 1985.

Charlesworth, James H. *The Old Testament Pseudepigrapha and the New Testament*. Harrisburg: Trinity Press, 1998.

Constable, Henry. *The Duration and Nature of Future Punishment*. London: Hobbs and Hammond, 1886.

Constable, Henry. *Hades, or the Intermediate State of Man*. Boston: Advent Christian Publications, undated.

Cook, Mary Alice. *Community of Grace*: *An Orthodox Christian Year in Alaska*. Chesterton: Conciliar Press, 2010.

Crockett, William. *Four Views on Hell*. Grand Rapids: Zondervan, 1992.

Crouse, Moses. *Modern Discussions of Man's Immortality*. Concord: Advent Christian Publications, 1960.

Cullman, Oscar. *Immortality of the Soul or Resurrection of the Dead?* London: Epworth Press, 1960.

Dean, David A. *Resurrection: His and Ours*. Charlotte: Advent Christian Publications, 1977.

Dean, David A. *Resurrection Hope*. Charlotte: Advent Christian General Conference, 1992.

Dean, David A. *The Gift from Above*. Charlotte: Advent Christian Publications, 1989.

Dickinson, Curtis. *Man and His Destiny*. Lubbock: Witness Press, undated.

Dickinson, Curtis. *What the Bible Teaches About Immortality and Future Punishment*. Alamogordo, 1984.

Edwards, David L. and Stott, John R.W. *Evangelical Essentials*. Downers Grove: InterVarsity Press, 1988.

Eliade, Mircea. *The Encyclopedia of Religion*. New York: Macmillan, 1987.

Field, Nathaniel. *A Debate on the State of the Dead*. Buchanan: Western Advent Christian Publishing Association, 1872.

Froom, LeRoy. *The Conditionalist Faith of Our Fathers*. Washington: Review and Herald Publishing, 1966.

Fudge, Edward. *The Fire That Consumes*. Houston: Providential Press, 1982.

Fudge, Edward. *Two Views of Hell*. Downers Grove: InterVarsity Press, 2000.

Gill, John. *The Cause of God and Truth*. London: W.H. Collingridge, 1855.

Goodspeed, Edgar. *Modern Apocrypha*. Boston: Beacon Press, 1956.

Graham, Billy. *Peace with God*. New York: Pocket Books, 1965.

Grant, Miles. *Positive Theology*. Boston, 1895.

Griswold, Millie (editor). *God's Prophetic Calendar*. Charlotte: Advent Christian General Conference, 1983.

Guillebaud, H.E. *The Righteous Judge*. Taunton: Phoenix Press, 1964.

Hagenbach, K.R. *A History of Christian Doctrines*. Edinburgh: T. and T. Clark, 1880.

Harris, Murray. *Raised Immortal*. Grand Rapids: Eerdmans, 1983.

Hastings, Horace. *After the Verdict*. Lenox: Himes Publications, 1982.

Hastings, Horace. *Pauline Theology*. New York: Copen Press, 1853.

Hatch, Sidney. *Daring to Differ: Adventures in Conditional Immortality*. Sherwood: Brief Bible Studies, 1991.

Hatch, Sidney. *Why I Believe In Conditional Immortality*. Portland: Advent Christian Press, 1961.

Hewitt, Clarence. *A Class Book in Eschatology*. Boston: Advent Christian Publications, 1942.

Hewitt, Clarence. *Faith for Today*. Boston: Warren Press, 1941.

Hewitt, Clarence. *The Conditional Principle in Theology*. Boston: Advent Christian Publications, 1954.

Hewitt, Clarence. *Vital Atonement*. Boston: Warren Press, 1946.

Hilborn, David. *The Nature of Hell*. Waynesboro: Paternoster Publishing, 2000.

Hoffman, Mark. *1989 World Almanac*. New York: Pharos Books, 1988.

Hone, William. *The Lost Books of the Bible*. Cleveland: World Publishing Company, 1948.

Hughes, Philip E. *The True Image*. Grand Rapids: Eerdmans, 1989.

Ives, Charles. *The Bible Doctrine of the Soul*. Philadelphia: Claxton, Remsen & Haffelfinger, 1878.

Lake, Kirsopp. *The Apostolic Fathers*. Cambridge: Harvard University Press, 1965.

Lewis, Eric. *Christ, the First Fruits*. Boston: Warren Press, 1949.

Lewis, Eric. *Life and Immortality*. Boston: Warren Press, 1949.

Lockyer, Herbert. *The Immortality of Saints*. London: Pickering & Inglis, Ltd., undated.

Lovett, C.S. *Death: Graduation to Glory*. Baldwin Park: Personal Christianity, 1974.

Mann, Cameron. *Future Punishment*. New York: Thomas Whittaker, 1888.

Mansfield, Mrs. E.S. *Adventual Essays*. Boston: Advent Christian Publications, 1893.

Marushchak, Archdeacon Vasiliy. *The Blessed Surgeon: The Life of Saint Luke Archbishop of Simferopol*, 2nd Edition. Manton: Divine Ascent Press, 2008.

Mbeke, Anne. *Clement of Alexandria and Conditional Immortality*. Charlotte: Venture Books, 2006.

McDonald, William. *The New Catholic Encyclopedia*. New York: McGraw-Hill, 1967.

McFarland, Norman. *Delivered From Death Unto Life*. Live Oak: Messenger Press, 1963.

Mead, Frank. *Handbook of Denominations in the United States*. Nashville: Abingdon Press, 1985.

Moyer, Elgin. *Wycliffe Biographical Dictionary of the Church*. Chicago: Moody Press, 1982.

Nichols, James A., Jr. *Christian Doctrines*. Nutley: Craig Press, 1970.

Osbeck, Kenneth W. *Amazing Grace: 366 Inspiring Hymn Stories for Daily Devotions*. Grand Rapids: Kregel Publications, 1990.

Palmer, A.C. *The One Fold and the Only Door*. Yarmouth: Scriptural Publication Society, 1885.

Pettingell, John H. *The Unspeakable Gift*. Boston: Advent Christian Publications, 1908.

Pettingell, John H. *Views and Reviews in Eschatology*. Yarmouth: Scriptural Publication Society, 1887.

Piper, Fred. *Conditionalism*. Boston: Advent Christian Publications, 1904.

Prestidge, Warren. *Life, Death and Destiny*. Auckland: Resurrection Publishing, 1998.

Roberts, Alexander. *The Ante-Nicene Fathers*. Ten volumes. New York: Charles Scribner's Sons, 1903.

Ryrie, Charles. *A Survey of Bible Doctrine*. Chicago: Moody Press, 1972.

Sabiers, Karl. *Where Are the Dead?* Akron: Rex Humbard Ministries, 1963.

Saint Herman Brotherhood. *Saint Herman Calendar* 2015. Platina: St. Herman of Alaska Brotherhood, 2015.

Schaff, Philip. *History of the Christian Church*. New York: Charles Scribner's Sons, 1903.

Schepps, Solomon. *The Lost Books of the Bible*. New York: Bell Publishing Company, 1979.

Schoolcraft, J. Ronald. *My Answers*. Kearney: Morris Publishing, 1994.

Schoolcraft, J. Ronald. *Woodman, Spare That Tree!* Kearney: Morris Publishing, 1992.

Sederquist, George W. *The Parting of the Ways.* Lynn: 1905.

Shedd, William. *The Doctrine of Endless Punishment.* London: James Nisbet, 1886.

Smith, Dustin. *Justin Martyr* (unpublished manuscript), 2006.

Stockman, E. A. *Our Hope, or Why Are We Adventists.* Boston: Advent Christian Publications, 1906.

Von Campenhausen, Hans. *The Fathers of the Greek Church.* New York: Pantheon Books, 1959.

Wellcome, Isaac C. *The Berean's Casket and Repository.* Boston: W.H. Pier & Co., 1869.

Whitmore, James. *The Doctrine of Immortality.* Boston: Advent Christian Publications, 1884.

Wierwille, Victor P. *Are the Dead Alive Now?* New Knoxville: American Christian Press), 1971.

Journals

Brandyberry, James. *The Development of the Doctrine of Immortality from the Apostolic Fathers to Augustine, Henceforth,* Volume XII, Number 1, 1983.

Fudge, Edward. *Journal of the Evangelical Theological Society,* Volume 27, 1984, "The Final End of the Wicked," 325–334.

Relevant Websites

www.carm.org/lostbooks.htm

www.ccel.org/fathers.html

Dr. John H. Roller

www.gnosis.org/library

www.iclnet.org/pub/resources/Christian-history.html

www.newadvent.org/fathers/index.html

www.voxdeibaptist.org/early_writings.htm

Early Christian Writings. *Abstract: The Odes of Solomon and Their Relationship with the Johannine Tradition and the Dead Sea Scrolls—* www.st-andrews.ac.uk/~www.sd/odessol.htm

Early Christian Writings: New Testament, Apocrypha, Gnostics, Church Fathers, *Odes of Solomon—*www.earlychristianwritings.com/odes.html

Early Christian Writings. *Supplementary Article No. 4: The Odes of Solomon—*www.pages.ca.inter.net/~oblio/supp04.htm

Wenham, John W. *The Case for Conditional Immortality—* http://www.truthaccordingtoscripture.com/documents/death/Wenham%20John%20-%20The%20Case%20for%20Conditional%20Immortality.pdf.

Acknowledgments

This book would not have been possible without the help of several institutions and individuals who assisted me in the research, writing, and compilation of the three distinct parts of the book.

Part I Data is a revision of my doctoral thesis, *The Doctrine of Immortality in the Early Church*, the research for which was mostly done in the Library of the University of Charleston (in Charleston, West Virginia), and which was presented to Bethany Theological Seminary (in Dothan, Alabama) in 1990.

Part II Application is a revision of my pastor-in-residence paper, *Advent Christian Church Planting Efforts 1950–1980*, the research for which was mostly done in the Adventual Collection room in the Library of Aurora University (in Aurora, Illinois). The Introduction to this Part is partially based on oral interviews with Mr. Thomas Lobb, of Aurora, Illinois, and Mrs. Helen Estep, of Charleston, West Virginia.

Part III Consequences was inspired by the contribution of Dr. Brian Keen, CGE.

The cover of the book was designed by Jean Keen, CGA, CPA.

My thanks to all of the above for their exceptional and invaluable assistance, and my apologies to any who contributed to the book in any way that I have neglected to mention!

www.ingramcontent.com/pod-product-compliance
Lightning Source LLC
Chambersburg PA
CBHW031937190326
41519CB00007B/569